Goetic Words of Power

Instant access to the Demons of the Goetia for Transformation, Power, and Success.

Tristan Whitespire

The Goetic Sigils in the center of the triangles are taken from Wikimedia Commons and therefore are not my work. The rest of the book was compiled by me from information gathered from many sources. Therefore, this book may be shared and distributed freely so long as the author is attributed.

Disclaimer: The information provided in this book is not to be taken for medical or professional advice under any

This book is dedicated to all of the authors of The Gallery of Magick. Without their inspiration this book would never have come to be. And to Och who illuminated my dense and foolish mind with divine revelation and insight. To my beautiful magickal family on the Facebook group. And finally, to Norma, my beautiful girlfriend by whose expertise with graphic design these sigils were made possible.

Introduction

Thank you so much for buying my book. I hope that you gain knowledge, wisdom, and understanding from the material that is presented here. To me, theory is useless unless it contributes to actual magickal results. Long and drawn out explanations in magick books bore me and so even though there is some theory to cover before getting to the magick, I will try to keep it to a minimum. Therefore, this introduction will be very short.

I first discovered magick when I was going through a particularly difficult time in my life. I was lost, lonely, and afraid. I didn't believe in magick or rituals and thought it was all a bunch of nonsense that had no power and didn't work. I decided out of desperation to try the rituals from The Mystic Grimoire of Mighty Spells and Rituals by Geof Gray-Cobb (which has now been rereleased by his wonderful daughter Vc-Toria Gray.) And I was blown away by the incredible energy I felt during the ritual. Results quickly followed that astounded me and continue to bear fruit for me till this day 8 years or so later. As a result of this experience I decided I wanted to know all there is to know about magick and rituals on my quest for spiritual evolution and the power to control my world.

Enter the Gallery of Magick. Most people reading this book will already know about Damon Brand and the Gallery of Magick. If you don't, do yourself a favor and go buy one of their books. You will not regret it. The Gallery of Magick is what led me to the place I am in today. With their brilliant simplification of complex magick and ingenious rituals I was able to discover just how simple magick could be while remaining effective. The value of the movement that they started in the magick and occult community is beyond human comprehension and I am convinced that the effects of their efforts will help carry this Earth into a Golden Age. But I digress.

Particularly, I was interested in Damon Brand's Words of Power. How could it be possible for simple words, quickly scanned and spoken, to create such immense and lasting change in our lives? I was left in the dark regarding this and gave up trying to find out the answer for many years.

RITUAL TO OCH

It has always been a desire of mine to become a writer but I never believed it to be possible. Just for fun and out of curiosity whether it would work or not (even though we are told by The Gallery of Magick repeatedly not to do magick just out of curiosity) I did a ritual to Och as seen in the book Chaos Magick by one of my favorite authors, Adam Blackthorne.

During the ritual I asked Och to give me the power to write books that inspire the hearts of others. I did not have magick books in mind at all. I was asking for the ability to write regular fiction novels. After the ritual things felt normal. Yet, a few days later I felt a sort of inspiration to begin to try reverse engineering Words of Power by Damon Brand.

I learned some Hebrew and took to the internet to try searching the names in the book. Many of the Hebrew names I searched kept bringing me to a book called The Book of Sacred Names by a brilliant author named Jacobus Swart. I purchased that book and discovered that a lot of the names found in Words of Power could be found in The Book of Sacred Names along with a detailed explanation of their powers and usage in magickal practice. The description of their powers aligned with the powers presented in Words of Power and everything clicked together for me.

Eager to try out my newly discovered knowledge I composed a few of my own rituals in the style of Words of Power and shared them to an amazing Facebook Group I am a member of. to my surprise and delight others felt the power of the words and began to have amazing experiences using them. I was hooked and doubled my researching to try to develop more magick. I loved being able to create something of value that benefited so many people for the first time in my life.

THE DEVELOPMENT OF GOETIC WORDS OF POWER

I quickly realized from my research that all magick is built upon words of power. If fascinated me how easily we could raise and direct potent spiritual forces to do our bidding with simply words and lightly focused intent. I noticed that a lot of people had been asking the Gallery of Magick to develop words of power that could be used to call upon the Goetic demons and became curious whether it would be possible.

Through my research I discovered that the preliminary words in a ritual evocation to the Goetic demons was primarily for 1, protection and 2, spiritual authority. So, I compiled words that would grant us protection, increase our spiritual authority, and also direct the energies to bring us a result quickly and reliably in a way that would bend time and space to bring us our desires.

DEVELOPMENT OF THE SYSTEM

This system that I present to you has never been seen before on Earth. The Goetic demons and 72 angels have been categorized astrologically before as can be seen through a quick search online but never before have they been categorized in the way that I present here. The differences in my system are numerous but one of the most obvious differences is that the traditional astrological attributions begin in Kether. I was led to begin the attributions in Chokmah.

I believe this method was given to me by divine revelation. Throughout the entire process it has felt more like I was receiving this information rather than creating it myself. Often, I would receive inspirations out of nowhere and ideas that would illuminate problems I had with the chart, providing insights without any prior research. Later, when I did research to confirm what I was being shown, my insights proved to be true and valid.

This is where I describe this system that has been revealed to me. This section also is not necessary to read. You can still use the powers and ritual as written and achieve the same results. The beauty of this system that has been revealed to me is that it liberates us from having to use and reuse the same old powers of the 72 demons, 72 angels, and 72 names of God as written in the old grimoires and allows us to discover our own powers for these spirits. But to do so we must understand what is called astrological aspects.

72 Rays of God

Yesod	Hod	Netzach	Tipareth	Geburah	Chesed	Binah	Chokmah	
Kahet 8 Kahetel Barbatos	Acha 7 Achahiah Amon	Lelah 6 Lelahel Valefar	Mahash 5 Mahashiah Marbas	Elem 4 Elemiah Gamigin	Sit 3 Sitael Vassago	Yeli 2 Yeliel Agares	Vehu 1 Vehuiah Bael	Chokmah
Hakem 16 Hakemiah Zepar	Hari 15 Hariel Eligor	Mebah 14 Mebahel Leraje	Yezel 13 Yezelel Beleth	Haha 12 Hahaiah Sitri	Lav 11 Laviah Gusoin	Elad 10 Eladiah Buer	Hezi 9 Heziel Paimon	Binah
Chav 24 Chaviah Naberius	Melah 23 Melahel Aim	Yeya 22 Yeyalel Ipos	Nelak 21 Nelakel Marax	Pahal 20 Pahaliah Purson	Lov 19 Loviah Sallos	Keli 18 Keliel Bathin	Lav 17 Lavel Botis	Chesed
Veshar 32 Veshariah Asmodai	Lekav 31 Lekavel Foras	Om 30 Omael Forneus	Riyi 29 Riyiel Astaroth	Shaah 28 Shahahiah Berith	Yeret 27 Yeretel Ronove	Haah 26 Haahiah Bune	Netah 25 Netahiah Glasya-Labolas	Geburah
Yeyi 40 Yeyizel Raum	Reho 39 Rehoel Malphas	Chaam 38 Chaamiah Halphas	Ani 37 Aniel Phenix	Menad 36 Menadel Stolas	Kevek 35 Kevekiah Marchosias	Lehach 34 Lehachiah Furfur	Yichu 33 Yichuiah Gaap	Tipareth
Mih 48 Mihael Haagenti	Eshal 47 Eshaliah Vuall	Ari 46 Ariel Bifrons	Sehahl 45 Sealiah Vine	Yelah 44 Yelahiah Shax	Veval 43 Vevaliah Sabnock	Mik 42 Mikael Vepar	Haha 41 Hahael Forcalor	Netzach
Poi 56 Poiel Gremori	Miv 55 Mivahiah Orobas	Nit 54 Nitael Murmus	Nena 53 Nenael Caim	Omem 52 Omemiah Alloces	Hachash 51 Hachashiah Balam	Dani 50 Daniel Furcas	Vehu 49 Vehuel Crocel	Hod
Machi 64 Machiel Haures	Anu 63 Anuel Andras	Yahah 62 Yahahel Valac	Umab 61 Umabel Zagan	Metzer 60 Metzerel Vapula	Harach 59 Harachel Orias	Yeyi 58 Yeyilel Amy	Nemem 57 Nememiah Ose	Yesod
Mum 72 Mumiah Andromalius	Hayi 71 Hayiel Dantalion	Yabam 70 Yabamel Seer	Raah 69 Raahel Decarabia	Chav 68 Chavuiah Belial	Iya 67 Iyahel Amducias	Menak 66 Menakel Cimeries	Damab 65 Damabiah Andrealphus	Malkuth

What you see in the previous chart is how the names of God are traditionally laid out. Reading from right to left, in 9 rows of 8 names. I was inspired to begin at Chokmah going down the right side and list the name of the sephiroth in order. The next one down would then be Binah, the next one down, Chesed, etc. This pattern continues down the right side until the last row, which is assigned to Malkuth.

I then was inspired to write the names of the Sephiroth across the top in the same way with Chokmah being the first box, Binah the second, Chesed the third, etc. across the top until the last box is assigned to Yesod.

I didn't understand why I was led to do this until I began to read up on the powers of each of the names of God as given in a wonderful chart that I discovered on this website: https://www.kabbalahinsights.com/en/products/digital-items It is the chart with the blue background. This chart lists the powers of each of the names of God in a way that I had never seen before.

As I read the names of God written on the poster and considered their powers in relation to their position on the chart I had been guided to create, I saw that to my surprise the powers matched their respective Sephirah perfectly! Each of the Sephiroth are ruled by a particular planet.

Chokmah = Neptune

Binah = Saturn

Chesed = Jupiter

Geburah = Mars

Tipereth = Sun

Netzach = Venus

Hod = Mercury

Yesod = Moon

At this point I realized how the chart worked. The names in each box revealed the combined powers of both names that intersected in the box. For example, box 1 is ruled by Chokmah and Chokmah. Box 2 is ruled by Binah and Chokmah. Box 20 is ruled by Chesed and Geburah, etc. So when you combine the planetary powers of each of the Sephiroth that rule that box and you compare it to the powers listed for the Name of God, angel, or demon you discover that their powers align with the combined influence of the 2 Sephiroth perfectly.

This is only possible to understand though when you have a detailed explanation of the powers of each spirit. For the names of God, I prefer the explanation of that chart I gave a link to above on the Kabbalah Insights website. For the powers of the 72 angels, I prefer the powers as listed in the book by Papus called The Qabalah. And for the 72 Demons surprisingly, the original Goetia book written in Olde English by Johann Wier in 1583 gives the most revealing description of their powers when using this system. Of course, you also cannot go wrong with Gordon Winterfield's amazing enlightening interpretation and of the powers of the 72 demons either.

ARIEL'S INSPIRATION

So, I thought that the entire system was complete until one day during a time I was working with the angel Ariel (#46) he whispered in my ear a single word, "trine". Now, I had no idea what that word meant so I do what any self-respecting person does when they encounter something they don't know, I Googled it! I was shown that there are three major astrological positions (actually 5 but trine/sextile and square/opposite are often combined since they are so similar in effect). The 3 positions are Conjunct, Trine/Sextile, And Square/Opposite.

Ariel showed me that the names of God are associated with the Conjunct aspect. The 72 angels are associated with the Trine/Sextile aspect. And the 72 Demons of the Goetia are associated with the Square/Opposite aspect. When I looked up the aspects on various websites, I discovered that it was true. The powers of the names, angels, and demons existed exactly with the powers associated with the planetary aspects to which they were assigned. This was a thrilling discovery for me and me at once knew I was onto something huge and revolutionary!

For example, the angel Menadel (#36) is associated with the Sun trine/sextile Mars position. Sun trine/sextile Mars people are passionate, determined, competitive, aggressive, hard-working, and confident. When we look up the powers of Menadel, we see that he brings courage, banishes fear, and helps us to work hard and retain our employment as well as liberating those who are in bondage, etc. His powers tie into that astrological position. This is just a brief example and I will be exploring this in more depth in future books.

BIRTH CHART AND PATRON NAMES, ANGELS, AND DEMONS

Further revelations continued from there. For example, I learned that we could use this information to discover our patron angels and demons based on the planetary aspects we held in our birth chart. If you want to discover your patrons right now you must first create your birth chart on this free website https://astro-charts.com/. Here you will be able to quickly create a chart that shows you what planetary aspects are present in your birth chart and from there you can simply match them up with the names on the chart.

Remember, there are three positions in each box. The top position is the Name of God and is associated with the Conjunct positions. The middle position is the name of the angel and is associated with the trine/sextile position. And the bottom position is the name of the demon of the Goetia and is associated with the square/opposite position.

Be aware that not all planets are covered in my chart. My chart covers the 8 basic planets. If you come across a planet that isn't covered in my chart, simply ignore it and move on to the next one. Perhaps in the future I will discover what matches with those other planets if anything. Maybe you will discover it. Who knows? This system is entirely new and is still developing so I am open to feedback and advice from readers.

Also, when it says, for example Saturn trine Sun, or Saturn sextile Sun, in this system it is the same thing. The same applies for square and opposite.

North Node

This is something that I did not invent but it is an idea that I haven't seen anyone else really talk about much. Your North Node shows you what your goal or mission is in this life. I am planning to write a book on this. This brief snippet might leave you a bit confused, but I am throwing this in there just to spark your imagination and ideas.

The North Node has three positions, called Decans. Each Decan has an angel, called Angels of the Decans. Because there are 12 possible North Nodes, 3 Decans for each node, there are of course, 36 Angels of the Decans. So, if your North Node is in Aries for example, you will have 3 Angels of that Decan that you may call on for aid and assistance in developing your mission in life. I intend to publish a book that lists all 36 Angels of the Decans including their powers and their associated tarot card that allows you to call on them.

I also intend to write a full book on finding your patrons that discusses the aspects more in depth and lists the corresponding Name of God, angel, or demon and discusses how they relate.

On an unrelated note, in my studies I was able to create a correspondence of the 72 Rays of God with the ancient Chinese Bagua. This one is very experimental, and I have hardly begun to understand all the implications of its correspondences, but I thought I would include it here for greater minds than my own to chew on and maybe make some sense of it.

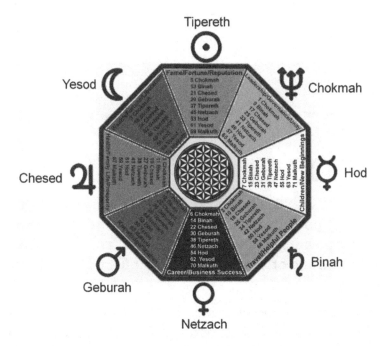

GOETIC WORDS OF POWER METHOD

When you work with Goetic Words of Power you are not only summoning the powers of the demon but you are also calling to your aid the powers of Names of God as well as angels such as Metatron, Raziel, and others that add great effectiveness to the ritual.

Some people also may be worried about calling on these demons without protection. Rest assured, this is one of my concerns as well. Coming from a Christian background I never quite let go of the fear of calling on supposed "demons", so I built extensive safety into the ritual itself. All the angels that one would call in the traditional protective circle ritual are included in the Goetic Words of Power. As you say the names you are simultaneously stepping into a field of divine authority to command spirits and a field of protection.

Because of this, you may or may not even feel the presence of the demon. Rest assured, the demons will hear you loud and clear and be ready to cooperate with you when you call to them using this method. The names you are calling on also are well known to bring you the favor of humans and spirits alike so using this method actually brings harmony to your physical and spiritual life on a number of levels and quite rapidly. So even if you don't immediately perceive the change you asked for, you will most likely notice your life flows more easily or you are in a much better mood than you were in previously.

If you are interested in learning the meaning and origin of the names buy Jacobus Swart's Book of Sacred Names. Also, for the names taken from the 72 Names of God, you will find their powers listed in Zanna Blaise's wonderful book 72 Sigils of Power.

I am obligated to state that any power you see here can be inverted and used for black magick. Which means that for the perceptive person, this entire book can be seen as an extensive grimoire of black magick. For example, we see that Agares under the 4th House of Home has the power to "Restore balance when our security in life has been destroyed." This means that he can also destroy security in someone's life so that they are thrown off balance. Anything that a spirit can do, they can also do the exact opposite.

The inspiration for the powers shown has been taken from this website http://www.astrology-x-files.com/transits/. As you can see if you care to browse that site, to discover the "astrological powers" of the demons in each house of the Zodiac, I have simply read what was on that page and wrote how the demon could solve the problem presented. So, if that website says, "relationships may be strained at this time," then I wrote that the demon has the power to, "heal strained relationships."

I appreciate when writers reveal their sources and tell how they discovered the powers for each spirit so here I am revealing my sources so that my readers can not only understand where I got the various powers that I list but also discover new powers on your own. That is the beauty of this system!

One of the most common questions when it comes to evoking spirits is how do we understand what powers the spirit has or how did the original writers discover the powers of the spirit? This system I present here for the first time in history (as far as I know) reveals how we can not only understand the given powers of a spirit on a deeper level but to discover and experiment with new powers for those spirits based on the planetary aspect they belong to!

When we work with spirits, we often fall into a rut of believing that the spirit only has a single power and isn't capable of more than is written in the grimoire about it. For example, if it says a spirit causes love between men and women, we think that the spirit is only good for causing love and maybe sex. Yet real life is never so cut and dried. Real people are never so one sided either.

I, for example, work at a contact center. If I was in a grimoire they may say I "aid in communication." But working at a contact center has also taught me about managing money, having discipline and patience, endurance, human psychology, how to get promoted in a corporation, etc. So, I could also teach others all of those things. It is the same with spirits we see in grimoires. In order to find their powers, we must contemplate their astrological position as shown in this system and read their traditional descriptions and imagine what other powers might be available to us from what we read there. This one paragraph can completely change your experience and understanding of working with spirits.

I am only touching briefly here on this because I will write more in depth on this in future books and may even host classes online that explains this information that has been revealed to me more in depth.

Here I will discuss very briefly the technique of using these calls. It is very easy to learn and apply. Each of the Goetic Demons has 4 angels that we call on before we call to the actual demon. Listed below the sigil of each demon you will find the names of the 4 angels as well as the name of the demon below them.

Be aware, the powers listed for each demon are only a suggestion. This ritual will work using any power ascribed to the demon from any system. This has been tested and proven to be true.

The first part of the call remains the same for each demon. Only the last 5 names change, that is, the names of the 4 angels, and of course the name of the demon. Here is an example of the ritual:

THE RITUAL METHOD
FOR GOETIC WORDS
OF POWER

1. Tune in to how you are feeling in your current state. Feel what brought you to this magick regardless of what it is. Breathe and tune into your current state of being.

2. Feel what your desire is and feel that sensation of lacking your desire. How does it make you feel emotionally? Allow those emotions to arise fully and without restrictions.

3. Begin to scan the sigil. Starting at the top middle (start at the Hebrew letter that the tip of the triangle is pointing to at the top of the circle), scan the outer circle counterclockwise. When done, scan the triangle starting from the bottom right, to the top of the triangle, then down the left side. Then right to left on the bottom.

4. Gaze at the sigil of the spirit in the center of the triangle and know that therein lies the power to resolve whatever problem you have. To fulfill whatever lack, you are feeling. This sigil is bursting with power to help you and a desire to do so. Feel a sense of gratitude welling up for that.

5. Say the words:

AH-DOH-NAI

EE-AH-OH

YICH-EH-AK-EV-CAH-HA

YITZ-OH-HAH-YAHV-TAH-HAH

YEE-YAH-HAH-GAV-LEE-HAH

GAH-DEE-YELL

TOO-VEE-YELL

OO-REE-YELL

RAH-FAH-EL

MEE-KAH-EL

GAH-BREE-YELL

YUH-DID-YAH

RAH-ZEE-YELL

YEH-OH-EL

NOO-REE-YELL

YAH-BAHM

EE-AH

OH-MEM

VEH-HOO

(the above names remain the same in every ritual so you may want to write them down on a separate sheet of paper or keep them on a separate screen to read them. The names below are the names of the four angels and the demon that will change with each ritual. In this case, for Paimon they would be):

HEH-ZEE-EL

HAH-EH-VAH-LEE-EL

ZEE-YEE-EL

YEH-NAH-EL

PAY-MON

(after saying these 5 names you would complete the rest of the ritual by saying the words below and changing only the name of the demon)

Hear me Paimon!

It is my will that you _____. (state your will 3 times in 2 sentences or less)

Paimon! I will give you public praise as a reward upon fulfillment. So that others may hear of your power and call upon you. Go in peace and cause no harm or loss to myself or my loved ones.

Hayah! Hoveh! Yiyeh! Shalom!

(and that is the end of the ritual.)

A note for those who are concerned about safety:

My intention was to build the protection into the ritual. All the angels in the Circle of Power ritual by The Gallery of Magick are in there. The name IAO is powerful for protection and controlling spirits. If those two things weren't enough, I also included a series of angels in here that correspond with a name of God that causes others (including spirits) to find you agreeable and to do your will. And finally (and perhaps most importantly) I included the angels that guide and restrain the demon. They are the names surrounding the triangle, the Shem angel and its emissary angels.

I also included the command that the spirit does not harm either us our loved ones or cause any loss to occur. I sealed all of that protection and power into this ritual with the words of power Hayah, Hoveh, Yiyeh, and Shalom (peace and harmony). So, in this ritual you have divine authority, angelic protection, the favor of humans and spirits, and a seal of divine peace built in. I'd say it's safe. But your experiences may vary so still, use your own judgments and use the magick at your own risk.

If you have any trouble or any questions regarding performing the rituals, I intend to start an online study group where we can share our experiences and talk about the rituals or ask questions.

1. BAEL

Planetary Aspect

Neptune square/opposite Neptune

Powers in the 12 houses

1st House of Self:

To raise low self-esteem.

To develop an attitude of confidence.

2nd House of Possessions:

To achieve financial clarity.

To perceive the true value of things we own.

3rd House of Communications:

To understand the message of another clearly.

To protect against being frauded or deceived.

4th House of Home:

To create understanding and acceptance in a family.

5th House of Creativity:

To cause a potential lover to see only aspects of yourself that are desirable to them.

To uncover your inner shadow so that it may be healed.

To come and go without being noticed (this does not give complete invisibility but puts a shadow around your aura so to speak so that you stand out less and are less memorable to those who see you. You also don't stick in people's memories as vividly).

6th House of Service and Health:

To bring stability during times of confusion in one's job.

7th House of Marriage and Partnership:

To reveal infidelity.

To conceal an affair.

To see the shadow side of a potential long-term.

8th House of Death and New Beginnings:

To discover unwanted parts of yourself such as bad habits or destructive thoughts and change them.

9th House of Mental Exploration:

To reveal hidden truths.

To reveal the true value of a spiritual teaching

10th House of Career:

To gain a clear vision of your current career path and change course to a more desired one.

11th House of Hopes, Wishes, and Friends:

To conceal group secrets.

To reveal the secrets of an organization to weaken them.

To uncover those who seek to undermine you.

12th House of the Subconscious, Dreams, and Secrets:

To create deep and fruitful states of meditation wherein much is revealed.

Words of Power

VEH-HOO-EE-YAH

VAH-VEH-LEE-EL

HAW-EL

VEH-NAH-EL

BAIL

2. AGARES

Planetary Aspect

Neptune square/opposite Saturn

Powers in the 12 houses

1st House of Self:

Bring clarity when you are unsure of who you are.

To reveal the true character of those in authority.

To give confidence and self-assurance.

2nd House of Possessions:

To learn how to manage one's money to enable financial stability and peace.

To protect one's possessions from theft.

To encourage another to repay money owed to you.

3rd House of Communications:

Restore communication with others when communication is broken.

Heal communication in a relationship.

Quiet negative inner dialogue to ease depression and anxiety.

4th House of Home:

Restore balance when our security in life has been destroyed.

To maintain peace in times of chaos and uncertainty.

To protect one's home against damage cause by people or natural disasters.

5th House of Creativity:

To give wisdom and insight to see the most profitable way to invest our time and money.

To inspire a romantic interest to see us as worthy of their time and attention.

To bring success to our projects and ventures.

6th House of Service and Health:

Bring strength to keep working when unwell.

To keep maintain focus and motivation on a project when others try to distract or demotivate you.

To understand the value of a current or potential relationship.

7th House of Marriage and Partnership:

To see our beloved for who they truly are, beyond our illusions of them.

To see the true character of others before our illusions of them cause us disappointment.

To understand who a good partner for us in business, marriage, or friendship would be.

8th House of Death and New Beginnings:

To cause our financial partnerships to be sound and profitable (banks, co-workers/co-owners of our company etc.)

To ensure our handling of money is accurate and balanced.

To satisfy to those who invest in us and ensure they feel rewarded.

9th House of Mental Exploration:

To bring clarity when one's deeply held beliefs are being challenged by contrary evidence.

Bring mental fortitude and strength to remain centered during paradigm shifts.

To understand and assimilate occult or philosophical teachings with clarity.

10th House of Career:

To protect your reputation when under scrutiny.

Maintain stability when others attempt to undermine your plans or reputation.

Help clarify the direction you wish your career or life path to take.

11th House of Hopes, Wishes, and Friends:

Enable smooth integration into groups or societies you wish to join.

Bring a clear shared vision to a group to enable harmony between all members.

To understand and clearly perceive current trends to stay "ahead of the curve" for the purpose of business success.

12th House of the Subconscious, Dreams, and Secrets:

To complete unfinished projects.

To bring resolution to unresolved issues from our past in any area of life.

To reveal those who plot against you.

Words of Power

YEH-LEE-EL

YAHT-EN-EE-EL

LEH-LAH-EL

YOH-EL

AH-GAR-EZ

3. VASSAGO

Planetary Aspect

Neptune square/opposite Jupiter

Powers in the 12 houses

1st House of Self:

To enable one to maintain clarity regarding their current situation in life.

To see through illusions and misconceptions to the reality of things.

2nd House of Possessions:

To clearly understand the status of our finances and what we can do to improve it.

To understand the true worth of things in our life.

3rd House of Communications:

To understand relationships for what they truly are without self-deception.

To cause others to feel compassion and generosity towards us.

Protect yourself from others taking advantage of you.

4th House of Home:

To understand the true needs of those who are close to us.

To clearly see and heal aspects of our psyche that weaken us and prevent us from being the best version of our self.

5th House of Creativity:

To see through illusions in our romantic partners.

To cause romantic interests to perceive us in a favorable light.

To inspire creative vision and recover lost passion and inspiration.

6th House of Service and Health:

To enable us to understand those we work with and work in harmony with them.

To see our mundane life clearly and for what it is. Facing the facts.

7th House of Marriage and Partnership:

To bring clarity to doubts and insecurities we have regarding an existing relationship.

To clearly see who someone is before signing a binding contract or entering into a long-term relationship with them.

To see clearly the best way to help those in need.

8th House of Death and New Beginnings:

To understand financial contracts with clarity before we sign them.

To see how to make joint ventures mutually beneficial for the parties involved.

9th House of Mental Exploration:

To enable understanding of occult texts, magick, and philosophy.

To enable clear vision and insight in regard to legal issues (may involve attracting the right legal professional to assist you).

10th House of Career:

To gain a clear vision for our career or life path.

To find space to take a step back and recuperate and reorganize our life.

To find the correct path once more when we go astray from our life's purpose.

11th House of Hopes, Wishes, and Friends:

To reestablish contact with lost friends or lovers.

To ensure clarity regarding our hopes, dreams, and wishes to avoid unrealistic expectations.

12th House of the Subconscious, Dreams, and Secrets:

To find space and time to find our true desires in our current life situation.

To bring clarity during times of soul searching.

Words of Power

SEET-AH-EL

SEET-EH-VAH-EL

YOH-FEH-FEE-EL

TOH-VEH-EE-EL

VAH-SAH-GOH

4. GAMIGIN

Planetary Aspect

Neptune square/opposite Mars

Powers in the 12 houses

1st House of Self:

To increase our personal levels of energy.

To aid in focusing our energies on whatsoever task we wish to accomplish effectively.

To appear as a confident and capable person

2nd House of Possessions:

To bring clarity regarding our finances.

To protect us from getting caught in scams.

To protect your money and possessions from theft.

3rd House of Communications:

To uncover the hidden agenda of others.

To be cause our communications to be clear and well received by others.

4th House of Home:

To see with clarity where we would best fit in and gain a sense of belonging.

To reveal secrets of those closest to us.

5th House of Creativity:

To bring happiness and harmony to an existing romantic relationship.

To bring confidence and initiative when gambling or investing in a way that make success more likely.

6th House of Service and Health:

To generate great drive, initiative, and motivation towards work and commitments.

To encourage another to pick up the pace when they are slacking and leaving the work for us.

7th House of Marriage and Partnership:

To reveal the secrets of our partners whether romantic, co-workers, etc.

To discover untruthfulness and unfaithfulness in those we partner with before it is too late.

8th House of Death and New Beginnings:

To protect against identity theft and misuse of our private information by others.

9th House of Mental Exploration:

To give us clarity, guidance, light, and wisdom during a "dark night of the soul."

10th House of Career:

Reveal those who seek to undermine our authority and position.

To keep our name clean and respected during times of scandal.

11th House of Hopes, Wishes, and Friends:

To reveal who in our life can be trusted and who we should be wary of.

12th House of the Subconscious, Dreams, and Secrets:

Inspire us with the energy we need to be outgoing and accomplish great things when we desire to give up.

Words of Power

EH-LEM-EE-YAH

AH-NEE-YEE-EL

LAHK-ME-EL

MEH-SHE-ASH-EE-EL

GAH-MEEG-IN

5. MARBAS

Planetary Aspect

Neptune square/opposite Sun

Powers in the 12 houses

1st House of Self:

To restore physical health, strength, and vitality

2nd House of Possessions:

Bring balance to the inflow and outflow of our finances.

To bring balance to our generosity to avoid giving too much.

3rd House of Communications:

To enable self-sufficiency in various aspects of life.

To ensure that our message is heard loud and clear when communicating

4th House of Home:

Encourage generosity from our parents in the form of money and favors.

5th House of Creativity:

To bring great creativity and enhanced imagination.

6th House of Service and Health:

To bring great health and strength.

To give us strength and endurance to excel at difficult jobs.

7th House of Marriage and Partnership:

To bring balance to our relationships with others.

To encourage both parties to contribute in all aspects of a relationship. Sexual, financial, and emotional.

8th House of Death and New Beginnings:

To encourage financial institutions to lend generously to our cause.

To increase generosity in others towards us.

9th House of Mental Exploration:

To gain a rich understanding of philosophy.

To encourage a rewarding experience when traveling to distant locations.

10th House of Career:

To stand out from the crowd and gain recognition from our superiors.

Inspire creative ideas in regard to our career path.

To contribute rewarding and valuable ideas in our job that can bring us reward and recognition.

11th House of Hopes, Wishes, and Friends

To bring self-knowledge through participation in group projects.

12th House of the Subconscious, Dreams, and Secrets:

To encourage clear and concise speech and self-expression when communicating with others.

Words of Power

MAH-HAH-SHE-YAH

MEE-KAH-EL

HAH-KOH-ZEE-EL

SHAM-EH-SHE-EL

MAR-BAHS

6. VALEFAR

Planetary Aspect

Neptune square/opposite Venus

Powers in the 12 houses

1st House of Self:

To cause others to perceive you as you wish to be perceived.

To encourage others to behave the way we wish them to without speaking to them.

2nd House of Possessions:

Enable us to perceive our finances with clarity to make necessary changes and adjustments as required.

To guard against extravagance and unnecessary overspending.

To protect against those who would swindle us out of money.

3rd House of Communications:

To have the courage to be direct in speech so that others understand our message with clarity.

4th House of Home:

Protect against those who would take advantage of us, draining our resources.

5th House of Creativity:

To bring great artistic inspiration.

To encourage a chance meeting that leads to romance.

6th House of Service and Health:

To encourage us to have the discipline to stay on schedule and be on time for work.

To appear as a good, diligent, reliable workers to those who employ us.

7th House of Marriage and Partnership:

To see a potential long-term romantic partner or marriage interest as they truly are to avoid disappointment later on.

8th House of Death and New Beginnings:

The gauge the true value of a potential investment.

To cause others to perceive what you present to them as valuable. Very useful to those in sales.

9th House of Mental Exploration:

To perceive the truth of a philosophy or teaching.

To enable an enjoyable and successful time when traveling to distant locations.

10th House of Career:

To bring clarity regarding your career path when others seek to influence your decisions.

To find great creativity and inspiration.

11th House of Hopes, Wishes, and Friends:

To see potential friends as they truly are.

To clarify our hopes, wishes, and dreams.

12th House of the Subconscious, Dreams, and Secrets:

To bring wisdom to moderate one's generosity to avoid being taken advantage of.

Words of Power

LEH-LAH-EL

LEH-LOO-ZEH-VAH-EL

LEH-LAH-EL

HAK-AH-LET-EE-YEL

VAH-LEH-FAR

7. AMON

Planetary Aspect

Neptune square/opposite Mercury

Powers in the 12 Houses

1st House of Self:

Enable you to express yourself clearly to avoid misunderstandings from others.

2nd House of Possessions:

To keep hold of one's financial assets and possessions when others seek to take advantage.

3rd House of Communications:

To enable one to be efficient and clear in actions and communications to avoid misunderstandings or accidents.

4th House of Home:

To give clarity regarding the true nature of contractual agreements before agreeing to them to avoid being scammed or swindled.

5th House of Creativity:

To discover great creative and artistic inspiration and expression.

6th House of Service and Health:

To ensure that communication between employers and co-workers remains clear and well understood to preserve harmony.

To bring healing.

7th House of Marriage and Partnership:

To guard against being swindled in regard to contractual agreements.

To heal relationships after they have been damaged.

8th House of Death and New Beginnings:

To bring understanding of how to change your personality to become the type of person you desire to be.

9th House of Mental Exploration:

To enable one to fruitfully explore and understand occult texts and philosophy.

Brings fruitful meditations on matters that confound you.

10th House of Career:

To protect one's public image and reputation when others seek to slander you.

11th House of Hopes, Wishes, and Friends:

To gain a full understanding of others beyond their appearances and actions. To understand the motives of others.

To uncover the truth behind the illusions those in our lives present to us to keep us in the dark.

12th House of the Subconscious, Dreams, and Secrets:

Enable restful sleep to restore our mind.

**Words of Power**

AH-KAH-EE-YAH

AH-DEH-VAH-REG-AH-EL

KEH-ROO-VEE-EL

AH-SHEH-SHE-EL

AH-MON

8. BARBATOS

Planetary Aspect

Neptune square/opposite Moon

Powers in the 12 houses

1st House of Self

To bring protection from receiving misinformation from those who desire to deceive you and lead you astray.

2nd House of Possessions:

To protect one from excessive spending.

Enable wisdom regarding financial balance and control.

To reveal those who drain your finances and protect you from them.

3rd House of Communications:

To protect from those closest to you such as family members who are a drain on your finances and seek to take advantage of you.

To keep you safe from the dangers untrustworthy people in your environment may bring upon you.

4th House of Home:

To encourage familial peace and a feeling of security in your home.

To encourage the generosity of family members and relatives towards us. Especially those we live with.

5th House of Creativity:

To cause the blossoming of romance.

To cause romantic interests to perceive us as we desire to be perceived.

6th House of Service and Health:

To protect from others stealing your ideas and taking credit for them.

7th House of Marriage and Partnership:

To encourage the reestablishment of balance in one-sided relationships.

8th House of Death and New Beginnings:

To encourage all parties involved in financial agreements to be honest and upholding their side of the bargain.

9th House of Mental Exploration:

To encourage prophetic visions of the future.

To increase psychic abilities in general.

10th House of Career:

To bring inspiration and creativity to your artistic pursuits.

To protect your reputation in regard to financial or work-related contracts and agreements.

11th House of Hopes, Wishes, and Friends:

To become a fountain of good will and giving that helps those that seek you out.

To encourage friends to be generous in lending to you.

12th House of the Subconscious, Dreams, and Secrets:

To restore emotional harmony in times of depression, angst, and instability.

Words of Power

KAH-HET-EL

KAH-NET-EE-EL

HAH-LESH-EE-YUH-MAH-EL

TOO-MEE-EL

BAR-BAH-TOHS

9. PAIMON

Planetary Aspect

Saturn square/opposite Neptune

Powers in the 12 houses

1st House of Self:

To bring self-confidence when the circumstances of life cause it to waver.

Brings courage to face any difficulty and meet any challenge directly without fear.

2nd House of Possessions:

To heal negativity caused by dark perceptions of the self.

To bring creative ideas that may lead to the generation of wealth.

3rd House of Communications:

Enhance one's ability to work with and learn new languages.

To enable clear, confident self-expression.

To enable clear and effective communication with the inner self/subconscious (enables us to change our patterns of behavior and habits on a deep level).

4th House of Home:

To enable families to communicate with each other clearly and peacefully.

5th House of Creativity:

To develop great skill in whatsoever art form we desire.

To bring great creative inspiration.

6th House of Service and Health:

To develop discipline that leads to personal growth and success.

To banish laziness.

7th House of Marriage and Partnership:

To enable a deep understanding of the needs and wants of our spouse or significant other.

To encourage togetherness and cooperation in a relationship.

8th House of Death and New Beginnings:

To encourage others to lend to us generously.

To transform our mind to enable the achievement of our goals.

9th House of Mental Exploration:

Brings understanding regarding any science, or occult philosophy.

To enable rapid learning.

To gain knowledge of the self.

10th House of Career:

To cause our superiors to admire us.

To make any person subject to our will and obedient to our desires.

11th House of Hopes, Wishes, and Friends:

To understand the mind of an organization or group of people to enable manipulation or assimilation.

12th House of the Subconscious, Dreams, and Secrets:

To shine a light on the darkness of the mind to banish fear and anxiety.

To encourage rapid recovery from addiction.

To break through inner darkness and move into the light of liberation.

Words of Power

HEH-ZEE-EL

HAH-EH-VAH-LEE-EL

ZEE-YEE-EL

YEH-NAH-EL

PAY-MON

10. BUER

Planetary Aspect

Saturn square/opposite Saturn

Powers in the 12 houses

1st House of Self:

To bring relief when your mind and emotions feel weighted down with concerns.

To encourage the restoration of health in mind, body, and spirit.

Gives strength when personal responsibilities seem too much to bear.

2nd House of Possessions:

To encourage saving money and frugality when one's tendency is to overspend.

3rd House of Communications:

To protect one from negative and depressing thoughts and emotions.

To gain a deep understanding of oneself.

To enable communication when the connection seems blocked.

4th House of Home:

To enable the resolution of old, persistent problems.

To find balance between social expectations and personal desires.

5th House of Creativity:

To bring back creative flow when creativity feels constrained and restricted.

To bring wisdom to investment decisions.

6th House of Service and Health:

To discover one's true desires beyond the grind of daily life.

To find relief when responsibilities are a heavy burden.

7th House of Marriage and Partnership:

To understand the true value of a current relationship.

To enable the resolution of disagreements.

8th House of Death and New Beginnings:

Encourage others to lend freely to us.

9th House of Mental Exploration:

To bring clarity regarding one's direction in life.

To remain resolute when one's beliefs are challenged.

10th House of Career:

To bring strength to handle responsibilities of our life when we feel overwhelmed.

11th House of Hopes, Wishes, and Friends:

To gain a clear vision of who is beneficial to your life and who is a burden.

To bring friendships and connections with those who encourage your growth and development in life.

12th House of the Subconscious, Dreams, and Secrets

To create space to breathe, meditate, and reenter oneself.

Words of Power

EH-LAH-DEE-YAH

OH-ME-EL

LAH-GEE-YEH-EL

DAW-DEH-LEE-EL

BOO-ARE

11. GUSION

Planetary Aspect

Saturn square/opposite Jupiter

Powers in the 12 houses

1st House of Self:

To restore energy and enthusiasm when one feels depressed.

2nd House of Possessions:

To enjoy life when resources are scarce.

3rd House of Communications:

To understand how to balance time alone with various obligations and responsibilities in our life.

4th House of Home:

To aid in finding a new apartment or house in which to live.

5th House of Creativity:

To restore richness to a relationship gone dull.

To release inhibitions that prevent freedom of self-expression.

6th House of Service and Health:

To bring strength to overcome obstacles and challenges that require hard work.

7th House of Marriage and Partnership:

To bring new life to a relationship that feels stale and routine.

8th House of Death and New Beginnings:

To enable powerful self-transformation through understanding of one's deepest self.

9th House of Mental Exploration:

To bring full understand of one's thoughts, mind, and beliefs to enable self-development.

10th House of Career:

To bring strength when one is overburdened with responsibilities in one's career life.

11th House of Hopes, Wishes, and Friends:

To enable time apart from friends where one may meditate and achieve new insight, perspective, and life direction.

12th House of the Subconscious, Dreams, and Secrets:

To bring wisdom regarding one's inner self.

Words of Power

LAH-VEE-YAH

LAH-TEM-EE-EL

OO-REE-EL

VAH-KEH-KEE-EL

GUSS-OH-EEN

12. SITRI

Planetary Aspect

Saturn square/opposite Mars

Powers in the 12 houses

1st House of Self:

To bring strength to accomplish all tasks required of us.

To bring self-confidence that others admire.

2nd House of Possessions:

To protect our finances and personal possessions from loss and theft.

3rd House of Communications:

To bring great ease in communication with others.

To enable mutual understanding in negotiations.

4th House of Home:

To bring balance and harmony between family members.

To ease communication in the home when it is strained.

5th House of Creativity:

To heat up a romantic relationship with passion when the fires of love have cooled.

To enable free and confident self-expression

6th House of Service and Health:

To bring strength to work in a consistent and focused manner to accomplish our goals.

7th House of Marriage and Partnership:

To bring harmony through sexual intimacy with a partner.

To encourage sexual desire.

8th House of Death and New Beginnings:

To encourage those who lend money to lend freely.

9th House of Mental Exploration:

To bring clarity regarding our direction in life.

10th House of Career:

To bring career direction and perspective.

11th House of Hopes, Wishes, and Friends:

To reignite and restore friendships that have gone stale.

12th House of the Subconscious, Dreams, and Secrets:

To soothe deep seated feeling of anger that burn us inside.

Words of Power

HAH-HAH-EE-YAH

HAH-VAH-EL

HAH-NEH-AH-VAH-EL

AH-SHEH-AH-SHE-YEL

SEA-TREE

13. BELETH

Planetary Aspect

Saturn square/opposite Sun

Powers in the 12 houses

1st House of Self:

To liberate our self-expression when we feel shy or inhibited.

To overcome those who seek to block us from achieving our goals.

2nd House of Possessions:

To enable one to save and spend money appropriately to avoid overspending.

3rd House of Communications:

To enable true self-expression when in the presence of others.

4th House of Home:

To bring harmony between friends and family.

5th House of Creativity:

To restore passion and love to our romantic relationships.

6th House of Service and Health:

To bring the strength and focus to work hard and accomplish much when tasks and responsibilities increase.

7th House of Marriage and Partnership:

To bring harmony to an imbalanced marriage so that partners see eye to eye and live in peace.

8th House of Death and New Beginnings

To encourage others to be more lenient and generous to you financially.

9th House of Mental Exploration:

Bring clarity and wisdom regarding one's direction in life.

10th House of Career:

To find relief when overwhelmed with responsibilities in the workplace.

To encourage employers to see you as strong, diligent, and capable to gain favor.

11th House of Hopes, Wishes, and Friends:

To encourage others to appreciate your creative talents.

To cause others to lend you a listening ear and give you consideration.

12th House of the Subconscious, Dreams, and Secrets:

To remain focused and have a clear minded when others try to draw you astray.

To cope with troubles that return to haunt us from the past.

Words of Power

YEH-ZEE-EL

YAW-FEE-EL

ZEH-VAH-EL

LAH-HEH-SHE-FEE-EL

BELL-ETH

14. LERAJE

Planetary Aspect

Saturn square/opposite Venus

Powers in the 12 houses

1st House of Self:

To bring great self-confidence.

To find relief from feelings of shame.

To increase popularity amongst friends and associates.

2nd House of Possessions:

To encourage satisfaction with what we own in our life.

3rd House of Communications:

To reestablish communication when barriers seem to be blocking it.

4th House of Home:

To encourage familial support and harmony.

To bring ease to a tense family situation.

5th House of Creativity:

To encourage the easy expression of romantic feelings without shame or shyness.

To open up and feel free when self-expression feels blocked.

6th House of Service and Health:

To encourage stronger connections and relationships with co-workers.

To bring enjoyment to mundane workdays.

7th House of Marriage and Partnership:

To restore frozen feelings in a marriage or long-term relationship so that love may blossom again.

8th House of Death and New Beginnings

To encourage generous lending of finances in our favor.

9th House of Mental Exploration:

To ease mental torment cause by negative thoughts and emotions.

10th House of Career

To increase popularity in the workplace.

To bring relief when responsibilities become overwhelming.

11th House of Hopes, Wishes, and Friends

To discover who your true friends are and to be rid of those who are not.

12th House of the Subconscious, Dreams, and Secrets

To break a period of solitude and welcome new friendships

Words of Power

MEH-BAH-EL

MAH-LEK-EE-EL

BOH-EL

HAW-KEH-EL

LEH-RAY-AH

15. ELIGOR

__Planetary Aspect__

Saturn square/opposite Mercury

__Powers in the 12 houses__

1st House of Self:

To be able to clearly express yourself

To clearly perceive important details in any matter or situation.

2nd House of Possessions:

To bring harmony and mutual understanding in financial discussions

3rd House of Communications:

To empower the mind to focus on whatsoever task we desire.

To create clarity and understanding in our communications with others

To perceive when opportunities open up that lead to success.

4th House of Home:

To increase feelings of harmony and belonging.

5th House of Creativity:

To restore romance in a relationship going stale.

To increase creative self-expression.

6th House of Service and Health:

To empower you to meet demands and deadlines at your place of work.

7th House of Marriage and Partnership:

To restore communication in a marriage such that both partners feel understood and accepted.

8th House of Death and New Beginnings:

To encourage generous lending from financial institutions.

To gain clarity regarding your finances.

9th House of Mental Exploration:

To restore connection and faith in the power of the universe.

To understand through contemplation, one's philosophy in life to enable spiritual growth and development.

10th House of Career:

To make important decisions regarding your career with wisdom and insight.

11th House of Hopes, Wishes, and Friends:

To restore lost connections with friends.

12th House of the Subconscious, Dreams, and Secrets:

To ease depression

To aid in self-discovery through contemplation.

__Words of Power__

HAH-REE-EL

HEH-VEE-YUH-VAH-EL

RAH-KEE-VAH-EL

YAW-NEE-EL

EL-EE-GOSS

16. ZEPAR

Planetary Aspect

Saturn square/opposite Moon

Powers in the 12 houses

1st House of Self:

To encourage emotional self-expression in our self or others.

To attract those who will banish our loneliness.

2nd House of Possessions:

To bring the strength to bring one's finances under control.

3rd House of Communications:

To encourage females to be especially supportive of you and desire to be around you.

To encourage freedom of expression of hidden or repressed emotions and desires.

4th House of Home:

To encourage a fulfilling period of life when life seems dull.

5th House of Creativity:

To encourage the expression of thoughts and emotions without fear, guilt, or shame.

To bring fire, passion and great sexual desire to romantic relationships or for purposes of seduction.

6th House of Service and Health:

To enable the enjoyment of our personal life free from undesired obligations for a short period of time.

7th House of Marriage and Partnership:

To encourage trust in a relationship.

To break down barriers to emotional expression in a relationship

8th House of Death and New Beginnings:

To encourage generous lending from financial institutions.

9th House of Mental Exploration:

To bring mental expansion and sharpening of the intellect.

10th House of Career:

To discover a career whereby one feels fulfilled.

To encourage others to hear us out and understand our views and opinions.

11th House of Hopes, Wishes, and Friends:

To bring supportive friendship.

To enable one to avoid those with whom one would rather not meet.

12th House of the Subconscious, Dreams, and Secrets:

To find relief from depression.

Words of Power

HAH-KEM-EE-YAH

HAH-KEE-MEE-EL

KAN-ET-EE-YAH-EL

ME-YUH-SHAH-AH-SHAH-EL

Tristan Whitespire

ZEP-ARE

17. BOTIS

Planetary Aspect

Jupiter square/opposite Neptune

Applications in the 12 houses

1st House of Self:

To break through delusions, we hold about our self.

To see our true potential.

To become our true self.

2nd House of Possessions:

To see the true value of a potential investment.

To understand any aspect of our financial life with clarity.

3rd House of Communications:

To see through lies that others tell us and recognize the truth.

To cause someone to reveal their true character.

4th House of Home:

To conceal a matter that we wish to keep private.

To find a new place to live that is in accordance with your desires.

5th House of Creativity:

To discover hidden talents.

To reveal the true thoughts and feelings of a romantic interest.

6th House of Service and Health:

To understand what direction, we desire our career to take.

To see what parts of our life are a burden that we can let go.

7th House of Marriage and Partnership:

To see the true potential of a long-term relationship.

To see a partner as they truly are.

8th House of Death and New Beginnings:

To bring necessary transformation when life seems stuck and stale.

9th House of Mental Exploration:

To undertake a period of self-study that brings great enlightenment.

10th House of Career:

To see the true nature of one in authority.

To be seen and appreciated by important people in our career field.

To find balance between your personal dreams and your career goals.

11th House of Hopes, Wishes, and Friends:

To find balance between social obligations and your productivity in your career.

To discern when one is being taken advantage of unfairly.

12th House of the Subconscious, Dreams, and Secrets:

To find balance between your inner and outer life.

To discover your hidden desires and needs.

To encourage others to reveal secrets.

Words of Power

LAH-VEL

LEH-OO-REE-EL

AHK-EH-MAH-SHE-EL

VEH-AH-LEH-AH-LEE-EL

BAH-TISS

18. BATHIN

Planetary Aspect

Jupiter square/opposite Saturn

Applications in the 12 houses

1st House of Self:

To gain clarity regarding one's path in life.

To find courage and self-confidence.

2nd House of Possessions:

To aid in the control of our finances.

3rd House of Communications:

For the clarity and wisdom to see new opportunities and take them.

4th House of Home:

To be free from the ties that hold us back from perusing our goals.

5th House of Creativity:

To bring wisdom to make wise investments of our time and energy.

6th House of Service and Health:

To bring stability when our life is undergoing major changes.

7th House of Marriage and Partnership:

To bring ease and harmony to our significant relationships.

8th House of Death and New Beginnings:

To allow us to change any aspect of our personality.

To remove bad habits or develop good ones.

9th House of Mental Exploration:

To organize and clarify our understanding of our spiritual worldview.

To cause others to see your point of view.

10th House of Career:

To make an important career decision with wisdom in a way that benefits our life.

11th House of Hopes, Wishes, and Friends:

To transform circumstances so that conditions are conducive to our success.

12th House of the Subconscious, Dreams, and Secrets:

To bring clarity regarding matters that confound you.

Words of Power

KEH-LEE-EL

KAW-KEH-VEE-EL

LEH-MEE-YUH-MAH-EL

YEH-MAH-NEE-EL

BAH-THEEN

19. SALLOS

Planetary Aspect

Jupiter square/opposite Jupiter

Applications in the 12 houses

1st House of Self:

To increase your popularity.

To increase popularity of a product or service you are offering.

2nd House of Possessions:

Helps to control our finances and prevents overspending.

3rd House of Communications:

To absorb and understand the material which we study on a deep level.

4th House of Home:

To bring harmony and peace to one's home life.

5th House of Creativity:

To encourage pregnancy.

To bring insight into investments.

To inspire creative ideas that may be financially profitable or bring popularity.

6th House of Service and Health:

To bring harmony and peace to our workplace relationships.

7th House of Marriage and Partnership:

To cause see others as they truly are.

To be seen as we truly are.

To bring understanding and mutual cooperation in the midst of differences of opinion and culture.

8th House of Death and New Beginnings:

To encourage a request for a loan to be approved.

9th House of Mental Exploration:

To undertake a period of soul searching whereby we gain insight and understanding into who we are.

To understand any philosophy and how it may be used to our benefit.

10th House of Career:

To bring career advancement without others feeling threatened.

11th House of Hopes, Wishes, and Friends:

To bring ease to times of great change in our life. To remain stable and strong.

12th House of the Subconscious, Dreams, and Secrets:

To see the truth of self beneath persistent thoughts and emotions.

Words of Power

LAW-VUH-EL

LAH-KEH-HAH-EL

VAH-FEE-EL

VEH-SAH-VEE-EL

SAH-LOHS

20. PURSON

__Planetary Aspect__

Jupiter square/opposite Mars

__Applications in the 12 houses__

1st House of Self:

To bring understanding of a situation through calm observation.

To avoid harm by undertaking projects that we cannot handle.

To understand our true potential regarding a project to decide if it will be a successful and profitable undertaking or not.

2nd House of Possessions:

To bring aid with saving money.

To reduce debt and increase gains.

3rd House of Communications:

To bring forth truth and resolution to a communal controversy.

To bring strength to face difficulties directly and overcome them.

4th House of Home:

To bring stability to an unstable home situation.

To ease relationships with parents or caretakers.

To bring harmony to our living situation.

5th House of Creativity:

To bring ease and peace to troubles in our romantic life.

To encourage luck and gains with gambling.

6th House of Service and Health:

To bring peace and harmony to one's work environment.

7th House of Marriage and Partnership:

To bring healing and harmony to a marriage.

To bring freedom and space to relationships that are overbearing.

8th House of Death and New Beginnings:

To encourage a request for a loan to be granted.

9th House of Mental Exploration:

To see through the hype and illusions that others present to try to convince you.

10th House of Career

To bring strength, drive, and willpower to successfully achieve promotion in your career.

To overcome those who seek to hinder your life and plans.

11th House of Hopes, Wishes, and Friends:

To enable easy adaptation during times of rapid change.

To bring stability and safety during times of upheaval and chaos.

12th House of the Subconscious, Dreams, and Secrets:

To clearly perceive the effect that your actions have on those around you.

Words of Power

PAH-HAH-LEE-YAH

PAHT-ZEK-EE-EL

HAH-DAH-EL

LEE-AH-HAH-EL

PURSE-ON

21. MARAX

**Planetary Aspect**

Jupiter square/opposite Sun

**Applications in the 12 houses**

1st House of Self:

To bring humility to oneself or others when blinded by ego.

To lead without being overbearing.

2nd House of Possessions:

To bring great financial gains through investing or by other means.

3rd House of Communications:

To put in their place those who overstep their bounds.

To see where in one's life there is room for growth and expansion.

4th House of Home:

To aid in relocating to a more peaceful and suitable dwelling that fits your needs.

5th House of Creativity:

To cause a romantic relationship to be steady and secure.

To bring wisdom to one's self-expression.

6th House of Service and Health:

To create a condition of mutual respect between our self and those we work with.

7th House of Marriage and Partnership:

To encourage balance and harmony in a long-term relationship.

8th House of Death and New Beginnings:

To cause others to see you as worthy of investment.

9th House of Mental Exploration:

To see the truth of the matter at hand with clarity and understanding.

10th House of Career:

To overcome obstacles that prevent promotion and career growth.

11th House of Hopes, Wishes, and Friends:

To discern with wisdom who is beneficial to associate with and who will be a burden.

12th House of the Subconscious, Dreams, and Secrets:

To see the truth of our self and gain a greater depth of understanding about our self.

Words of Power

NEH-LAH-KEL

NEH-MOO-EL

LAH-MEH-SEE-EL

KEH-SEE-GAH-EL

MAH-RAHZ

22. IPOS

__Planetary Aspect__

Jupiter square/opposite Venus

__Applications in the 12 houses__

1st House of Self:

To develop discipline.

To develop willpower and confidence.

2nd House of Possessions:

To learn to handle one's finances in a wise manner.

3rd House of Communications:

To bring harmony to a troublesome relationship.

4th House of Home:

To create an aesthetically pleasing home.

To find a new place to live that is within budget.

5th House of Creativity:

To bring balance and equality to a relationship.

6th House of Service and Health:

To cause others to see you as likeable.

To cause others to be willing to understand you and see your side of things.

7th House of Marriage and Partnership:

To bring back a partner who strays.

8th House of Death and New Beginnings:

To reach new levels of success in whatsoever one wishes.

9th House of Mental Exploration:

To cause others to see you as a trustworthy person.

10th House of Career:

To encourage others to help bring about your desired goals.

To see clearly those who desire to use you for their own gains.

11th House of Hopes, Wishes, and Friends:

To create a sense of belonging wheresoever you are.

12th House of the Subconscious, Dreams, and Secrets:

To overcome those who try pressuring you to give them what they desire at your expense.

Words of Power

YEH-YAH-EE-EL

YAH-AH-LEE-EL

YEH-HAW-HEE-EL

YAHTZ-EE-YUH-VAH-EL

EE-POSE

23. AIM

Planetary Aspect

Jupiter square/opposite Mercury

Applications in the 12 houses

1st House of Self:

To express oneself clearly and directly without being seen as rude or inappropriate.

2nd House of Possessions:

To bring great fortune to your business endeavors.

3rd House of Communications:

To enhance one's ability to learn quickly and absorb information. Good for test taking.

4th House of Home:

To discover hidden secrets.

To find contentment with your current settings.

5th House of Creativity:

To enable a period of great creative productivity.

To discover hidden talents.

To express oneself fully in whatsoever is undertaken.

6th House of Service and Health:

To ease feelings of nervousness.

To work clearly and accurately to avoid making mistakes.

7th House of Marriage and Partnership:

To bring mutual understanding and harmony to a marriage or long-term relationship.

8th House of Death and New Beginnings:

To aid in understanding how best to consolidate one's debts.

9th House of Mental Exploration:

To find one's way when lost. Figuratively or literally.

10th House of Career:

To maintain one's reputation when others seek to slander you by spreading lies.

11th House of Hopes, Wishes, and Friends:

To harmonize with different groups of people and work together towards a mutually beneficial goal.

12th House of the Subconscious, Dreams, and Secrets:

To cause others to reveal secrets about themselves during conversation.

To see yourself and your potential clearly and without delusion.

Words of Power

MEH-LAH-EL

MEH-ZAH-KEY-EL

LEH-LAH-EL

HAW-KEG-EE-ELL

AY-MM

24. NABERIUS

Planetary Aspect

Jupiter square/opposite Moon

Applications in the 12 houses

1st House of Self:

To develop discipline.

2nd House of Possessions:

To bring balance to one's finances and wisdom to avoid debt.

3rd House of Communications:

To keep secrets concealed.

4th House of Home:

To encourage others to support you.

5th House of Creativity:

To encourage childbirth.

To find a romantic relationship.

6th House of Service and Health:

To restore boundaries when others impose and expect too much of you.

7th House of Marriage and Partnership:

To create balance and equality in a relationship.

8th House of Death and New Beginnings:

To find within oneself the strength, initiative, and willpower one needs to accomplish a desired task. Or to increase these qualities generally.

9th House of Mental Exploration:

To bring understanding to our relationships with others.

To bring peace and calmness to one's mind and encourage peaceful sleep.

10th House of Career:

To encourage career advancement to a position of authority.

11th House of Hopes, Wishes, and Friends:

To encourage people around us to support our dreams and aspirations to help us achieve our goals.

12th House of the Subconscious, Dreams, and Secrets:

To produce a time of fruitful meditation and quiet reflection to bring about desired changes in one's life.

Words of Power

KAH-WHO-EE-AH

KAH-NEE-EL

HAW-FEE-NEE-EL

VESH-AH-AH-SHE-EL

NAH-BEH-REE-US

25. GLASYA-LABOLAS

Planetary Aspect

Mars square/opposite Neptune

Applications in the 12 houses

1st House of Self:

To develop self-confidence.

2nd House of Possessions:

To see which investments of our time and/or money would be most profitable.

3rd House of Communications:

To have the wisdom to know what to say in communication with others to achieve our goals.

4th House of Home:

To receive sound advice and wise counsel

5th House of Creativity:

To bring clarity regarding the best actions to take in a given situation.

6th House of Service and Health:

To bring understanding between our self and those we work with.

To increase personal energy and strength when we feel weak or impotent.

7th House of Marriage and Partnership:

To understand the needs of a partner and how to best fulfill them.

8th House of Death and New Beginnings

To bring the wisdom to choose a new direction in our life.

9th House of Mental Exploration:

To discern who is telling us the truth and who is lying to us for their own gains.

10th House of Career

To understand the best career path to take.

11th House of Hopes, Wishes, and Friends

To understand the motivations and desires of those who are closest to us.

12th House of the Subconscious, Dreams, and Secrets

To understand the direction that our life is going and how to change that direction if desired.

Words of Power

NET-AH-EE-AH

NOO-ME-EL

TAH-TEE-VAH-EL

HAW-NEH-NEE-EL

GLAH-SEE-AH LAH-BOW-LAHS

26. BUNE

Mars square/opposite Saturn

Applications in the 12 houses

1st House of Self:

To hold your ground and be unmovable by those who seek to influence you or rush you to a decision.

2nd House of Possessions:

To bring great financial fortune.

3rd House of Communications:

To understand what to say and speak with great dignity, eloquence, and wisdom.

4th House of Home:

To find a place to live that is affordable and pleasing to us.

5th House of Creativity:

To bring wisdom to make appropriate financial decisions.

6th House of Service and Health:

To bring strength when one's work situation wears you down.

7th House of Marriage and Partnership:

To develop patience in a relationship.

To restore proper communication in a relationship.

8th House of Death and New Beginnings:

To end procrastination.

9th House of Mental Exploration:

To inspire hope.

To find the words to say when trying to express a matter of importance.

10th House of Career:

To bring about a promotion.

11th House of Hopes, Wishes, and Friends:

To rise above loneliness and meet others who charm you.

12th House of the Subconscious, Dreams, and Secrets:

To bring those things that hinder us to the light to be released and healed.

Words of Power

HAH-AH-EL

HAH-AH-MEE-EL

AH-DEH-MEE-EL

AH-BAH-EL

BOON

27. RONOVE

Planetary Aspect

Mars square/opposite Jupiter

Applications in the 12 houses

1st House of Self:

To be considerate and understanding towards others.

To protect against accidents.

2nd House of Possessions:

To avoid overspending.

3rd House of Communications:

To give strength to cope with a hectic schedule.

4th House of Home:

To bring peace during a stressful and chaotic time.

To smoothly transition to a new home.

5th House of Creativity:

To ignite romantic passion in an existing relationship.

To bring a new romantic relationship into your life.

6th House of Service and Health:

To get along well with one's coworkers.

To make peace with one's superiors at work.

7th House of Marriage and Partnership:

To resolve misunderstandings with a current partner and bring mutual understanding.

8th House of Death and New Beginnings:

To ensure those who seek us for our money do not overstep their bounds.

9th House of Mental Exploration:

To aid one in being victorious during a lawsuit or trial in court.

10th House of Career:

To allow one's career ambitions to be successfully fulfilled.

11th House of Hopes, Wishes, and Friends:

To bring protection when one is surrounded by controversy.

Brings intuition to recognize good and bad advice one receives from others.

12th House of the Subconscious, Dreams, and Secrets:

To bring silence to a controversy.

To bring contentment with one's current circumstances to enable greater things to flow into one's life.

Words of Power

YEH-REH-TEL

YOO-NEH-NEE-EL

RAH-KAH-ZEE-EL

TAH-TEH-VEE-EL

ROW-NO-VEH

28. BERITH

Planetary Aspect

Mars square/opposite Mars

Applications in the 12 houses

1st House of Self:

To calm anger and irritation in oneself or others.

To develop self-confidence.

To bring peace to feelings of anxiety.

To bring the strength, energy, and discipline to exercise.

2nd House of Possessions:

To enable one to make wise financial decisions.

3rd House of Communications:

To bring peace to arguments.

To bring safety and protection from accidents during travel.

4th House of Home:

To overcome adversity through decisive action.

To bring peace during a chaotic time.

5th House of Creativity:

To express oneself clearly, concisely, and with wisdom.

To be victorious over those who are unfair and deceitful.

6th House of Service and Health:

To get much done in a short time.

Bring the wisdom to make important career decisions.

7th House of Marriage and Partnership:

To cause a breakthrough when one's relationship is troubled or stale (this has the effect of either ending the relationship or it will undergo a positive transformation).

8th House of Death and New Beginnings:

To bring financial stability during dangerous and unstable times.

9th House of Mental Exploration:

To enable discussions on delicate or difficult topics in a clear headed and rational manner.

To encourage mutual understanding to end a debate.

10th House of Career:

To bring a promotion at work.

To discover a new, more satisfying career.

11th House of Hopes, Wishes, and Friends:

To bring strength and success to your ambitions to acquire whatsoever you desire.

12th House of the Subconscious, Dreams, and Secrets:

To protect oneself against those who seek to deceive you.

To see through lies.

Words of Power

SHAH-AH-EE-AH

SHAW-ME-EL

AH-HAH-REH-VEE-EL

HAH-GEH-TAH-ME-EL

BEH-RITH

29. ASTAROTH

Planetary Aspect

Mars square/opposite Sun

Applications in the 12 houses

1st House of Self:

To encourage others to go along with your plans without complaints.

To bring an atmosphere of cooperation and harmony in a group.

2nd House of Possessions:

To protect one's possessions from being damaged.

To guard against excessive expenses.

3rd House of Communications:

To allow for smooth and harmonious communication with others.

To speak one's mind without causing offense.

4th House of Home:

To bring the wisdom to make an important decision.

5th House of Creativity:

To be victorious in competition.

To develop great strength, willpower, and determination to accomplish one's goals.

6th House of Service and Health:

To give the strength to endure hard work.

7th House of Marriage and Partnership:

To bring harmony to one's long term relationships.

8th House of Death and New Beginnings:

To encourage others to lend freely.

To bring wisdom regarding important financial decisions.

9th House of Mental Exploration:

To bring the courage to stand firm when one's integrity or beliefs are challenged.

10th House of Career:

To get a promotion to a position of leadership and authority in one's career.

To cause others to support and respect your authority.

11th House of Hopes, Wishes, and Friends:

To bring social peace and harmony.

To see who may or may not be trusted.

12th House of the Subconscious, Dreams, and Secrets:

To understand the best action to take when faced with a troubling situation.

Words of Power

REE-EE-EL

RAH-SHEN-EE-EL

YAH-FEE-NEE-EL

YAH-KEK-EE-ME-EL

AHS-TAR-OTH

30. FORNEUS

Planetary Aspect

Mars square/opposite Venus

Applications in the 12 houses

1st House of Self:

To cause others to admire you.

To bring personal popularity.

2nd House of Possessions:

To bring the discipline to avoid wasteful habits.

3rd House of Communications:

To encourage chance meetings.

To encourage a fruitful time of creative and artistic expression.

4th House of Home:

To bring privacy to oneself or a situation.

5th House of Creativity:

To encourage a chance meeting with a new romantic partner.

To bring excitement to one's dull sexual life.

6th House of Service and Health:

To bring the focus to accomplish one's work without distraction.

7th House of Marriage and Partnership:

To bring harmony and balance to a long-term relationship or marriage.

8th House of Death and New Beginnings:

To bring balance and harmony to one's financial management.

9th House of Mental Exploration:

To find love online.

To maintain a long-distance relationship.

10th House of Career:

To stop jealousy in oneself or others.

To overcome those who stand in the way of your career success.

11th House of Hopes, Wishes, and Friends:

To resolve awkward situations, you find yourself in.

12th House of the Subconscious, Dreams, and Secrets:

To bring secrecy to an affair so that it remains hidden.

Words of Power

AW-MUH-EL

ASH-EF-EE-YEL

VEH-NAH-EH-DEE-EL

MEM-AH-YEL

FOR-NAY-US

31. FORAS

Planetary Aspect

Mars square/opposite Mercury

Applications in the 12 houses

1st House of Self:

To stand firm when one's position is challenged.

To bring victorious resolution to arguments.

2nd House of Possessions:

To bring stability and wisdom to one's financial decisions and management.

3rd House of Communications:

To bring a peaceful resolution to arguments.

4th House of Home:

To restore peace to one's home during troubled times.

5th House of Creativity:

To express oneself clearly and effectively.

To bring peace to arguments with our lover.

6th House of Service and Health:

To bring peace and order during times of anxiety or chaos at work.

7th House of Marriage and Partnership:

To bring harmony and mutual understanding in a relationship during arguments.

8th House of Death and New Beginnings:

To uncover hidden talents.

9th House of Mental Exploration:

To bring peace to arguments.

To allow for fruitful outcomes to debates.

10th House of Career:

To protect one's reputation at work.

To eloquently defend oneself when challenged.

11th House of Hopes, Wishes, and Friends:

To expand one's social circle and make new friends.

12th House of the Subconscious, Dreams, and Secrets:

To bring wisdom to make an important decision.

To understand the true intentions behind the words and actions of others.

Words of Power

LEH-KAHV-EL

LEH-SHAH-AH-VET-EE-YEL

KAH-TEH-VEE-YEL

VAH-NEH-TEE-YEL

FOE-RAHS

32. ASMODAI

Planetary Aspect

Mars square/opposite Moon

Applications in the 12 houses

1st House of Self:

To bring the wisdom to make important decisions regarding one's personal life.

To bring wisdom to act appropriately in any situation.

2nd House of Possessions:

To protect against financial losses.

To manage one's finances and budget to enable the achievement of goals.

3rd House of Communications:

To overcome bad habits.

To see others and situations as they truly are to enable responsible and appropriate decisions to be made.

4th House of Home:

To see a way out of difficult or overwhelming circumstances to that a fresh start can be made.

5th House of Creativity:

To stop jealousy in one's romantic life.

To bring wisdom to make wise investments.

To bring peace to situations regarding one's romantic life.

6th House of Service and Health:

To be maintain good health and strength during stressful times.

7th House of Marriage and Partnership:

To bring peace to one's marriage.

To create space in a relationship to work out disagreements.

8th House of Death and New Beginnings:

To bring harmony to one's finances.

9th House of Mental Exploration:

To defend one's thoughts, beliefs and works of art against critics.

10th House of Career:

To find a balance between one's career and personal life.

To overcome the competition for a coveted promotion.

To encourage one's superiors to be lenient with you.

11th House of Hopes, Wishes, and Friends:

To bring harmony to relationships with friends and acquaintances.

12th House of the Subconscious, Dreams, and Secrets:

To bring peace to one's emotions.

To bring peace of mind.

To release the past.

Words of Power

VESH-EE-REE-AH

VAH-VEH-LEE-EL

SHAH-MEH-SHE-EL

RAH-KAH-VEE-EL

AHZ-MOH-DAY

33. GAAP

Planetary Aspect

Sun square/opposite Neptune

Applications in the 12 houses

1st House of Self:

To bring clarity when your life seems confused.

2nd House of Possessions:

To enable wise financial decisions to be made.

3rd House of Communications:

To bring clear understanding of the reasons behind the words and actions of others.

4th House of Home:

To bring understanding between members of a family.

5th House of Creativity:

To bring creative inspiration and vision.

To inspire love in another person for us.

6th House of Service and Health:

To bring the courage to face one's work directly even when it seems overwhelming.

7th House of Marriage and Partnership:

To bring clarity and understanding to communication with partners.

8th House of Death and New Beginnings:

To bring relief and a pathway of escape during troublesome situations.

9th House of Mental Exploration:

To discover one's spiritual path.

10th House of Career:

To understand what moves to make to achieve one's career goals.

11th House of Hopes, Wishes, and Friends:

To see a clear path towards the achievement of one's dreams.

12th House of the Subconscious, Dreams, and Secrets:

To bring clarity when a situation is confusing.

Words of Power

YEE-KOO-EE-AH

YAH-REH-VEE-EE-EL

KAW-KEM-EE-EL

VESH-ADD-EE-EL

GAHP

34. FURFUR

Planetary Aspect

Sun square/opposite Saturn

Applications in the 12 houses

1st House of Self:

To bring clarity to one's life path.

To defend oneself when one's authority is questions.

To connect with others when one feels alone.

2nd House of Possessions:

To bring resolution to financial troubles.

For aid resolving debts.

3rd House of Communications:

To bring safety and ease while traveling.

To bring strength when responsibilities weigh you down.

4th House of Home:

To find a way to balance leisure with responsibility.

5th House of Creativity:

To bring fortune to financial investments.

To bring warmth and genuine feelings back to a relationship that has become stale and routine.

6th House of Service and Health:

To stand up to scrutiny at one's place of work and come out on top.

7th House of Marriage and Partnership:

To see flaws in a current relationship clearly for the purpose of correcting them.

To gain the cooperation of others.

8th House of Death and New Beginnings

To enable your money to go further.

9th House of Mental Exploration:

To be skeptical but keep an open mind.

To stand strong when one's faith is tested.

10th House of Career:

To cause your authority to be acknowledged and respected.

11th House of Hopes, Wishes, and Friends:

To overcome those who stand it the way of the achievement of your goals.

12th House of the Subconscious, Dreams, and Secrets:

To end procrastination.

To bear the weight of responsibility without slowing down.

Words of Power

LEH-HAH-KEY-AH

LAH-SHEK-EE-YEL

HAG-ET-EE-EL

KAHT-EM-EE-EATZ-AH-EL

FUR-FUR

35. MARCHOSIAS

Planetary Aspect

Sun square/opposite Jupiter

Applications in the 12 houses:

1st House of Self:

To make a good impression on others naturally and with ease.

To avoid creating enemies while accomplishing your goals.

2nd House of Possessions:

To bring wisdom to invest wisely.

3rd House of Communications:

To ensure that issues are swiftly resolved and do not turn into a big deal.

4th House of Home:

To improve one's relationship with parents.

5th House of Creativity:

To bring good luck.

To bring peace and security to one's romantic relationships.

To bring fortune to investments.

6th House of Service and Health:

To maintain strength and discipline when on a diet.

To bring good fortune to one's work life.

To bring harmony to relationships with our managers and employers.

7th House of Marriage and Partnership:

To bring equality and harmony to a relationship.

8th House of Death and New Beginnings

To bring focus and drive to accomplish one's ambitions.

9th House of Mental Exploration:

To overcome and achieve victory during power struggles.

10th House of Career:

To bring easy advancement in one's career.

11th House of Hopes, Wishes, and Friends:

To attract a mentor who can bring success to your goals.

12th House of the Subconscious, Dreams, and Secrets:

To enable a period of rest, recuperation, and ease.

Words of Power

KEV-EK-EE-AH

KAHTZ-ET-EE-YEL

VAH-TEK-EE-YEL

KOO-ME-YEL

MAR-KOH-SEE-AHS

36. STOLAS

__Planetary Aspect__

Sun square/opposite Mars

__Applications in the 12 houses__

1st House of Self:

Bring the strength and motivation to exercise.

To stay strong and face conflict with others head on and fear-lessly.

2nd House of Possessions:

To bring wisdom to make important financial decisions.

3rd House of Communications:

To enable clear and effective communication with others.

4th House of Home:

To bring peace and stability to one's home life.

5th House of Creativity:

To bring wisdom to make wise investment decisions.

To bring peace to our romantic relationships.

6th House of Service and Health:

Bring wisdom to make important decisions regarding our place of employment.

To understand how to bring resolution to a situation at work that angers us.

7th House of Marriage and Partnership:

Cause our employers to see us as reliable.

To see clearly what isn't working in our relationships with others and the wisdom to resolve it.

8th House of Death and New Beginnings

To bring drive and willpower to accomplish the goals one sets for oneself.

9th House of Mental Exploration:

To resolve arguments and disagreements on matters of thought and philosophy as well as law.

10th House of Career:

To bring career success and advancement.

11th House of Hopes, Wishes, and Friends:

To obtain the cooperation of those with whom we work or are closely associated with.

12th House of the Subconscious, Dreams, and Secrets:

To be made safe from being led astray by those around us.

To keep our intentions from being known by others.

Words of Power

MEN-AH-DEL

MAH-LEK-EE-YEL

NAH-DEN-EE-YEL

DAHS-EL-EE-YEL

STOW-LAHS

37. PHENIX

Planetary Aspect

Sun square/opposite Sun

Applications in the 12 houses

1st House of Self:

Go gain the cooperation of others in our pursuits.

2nd House of Possessions:

To gain wisdom on managing our investment activities.

3rd House of Communications:

To see an issue from a higher perspective to enable wisdom to make the best decision.

4th House of Home:

To bring balance to one's career and domestic life.

5th House of Creativity:

To express oneself in a careful way that does not offend others.

6th House of Service and Health:

To bring the strength to manage a stressful and demanding time at work.

To cause our employer to be less demanding of us.

7th House of Marriage and Partnership:

To encourage cooperation and clear communication with a work or romantic partner.

8th House of Death and New Beginnings:

To bring confidence and clarity to our finances.

To raise our self-esteem

9th House of Mental Exploration:

To see an issue from a wider perspective.

10th House of Career:

To plan for a secure and successful career path or retirement.

To bring harmony and cooperation with those who employ us.

11th House of Hopes, Wishes, and Friends:

To hear and understand the desires of others clearly.

To encourage the cooperation of others.

12th House of the Subconscious, Dreams, and Secrets:

To end procrastination.

Words of Power

AH-NEE-EL

AHK-EH-ZEE-EEN-EE-YEL

NEE-YEEN-EH-NAH-EL

YEH-DEH-EE-YEL

FIH-NICKS

38. HALPHAS

__Planetary Aspect__

Sun square/opposite Venus

__Applications in the 12 houses__

1st House of Self:

To focus on self-creation. Building one's style and shaping one's personality to be what one desires.

2nd House of Possessions:

To bring aid to one's financial life.

To invest wisely.

3rd House of Communications:

To bring harmony to communication when personalities or viewpoints may clash.

4th House of Home:

To bring industriousness to combat one's tendencies towards laziness.

To maintain boundaries and keep others from intruding.

5th House of Creativity:

To avoid overspending.

To experience and enjoyable time during social occasions and gatherings.

6th House of Service and Health:

To encourage mutual understanding and cooperation between coworkers.

7th House of Marriage and Partnership:

To bring mutual cooperation and understanding to a relationship when differences in desire calls for a compromise.

8th House of Death and New Beginnings:

To prevent overspending.

To gain the energy to fight tendencies towards laziness and accomplish our goals.

9th House of Mental Exploration:

To be mindful of the culture, ideas, or preferences of others to avoid stepping over boundaries and causing offense.

10th House of Career:

To accomplish much without being seen.

To move about in secrecy to enable great effectiveness.

Give strength to stand up to the demands of our superiors.

11th House of Hopes, Wishes, and Friends:

To bring ease to social and political tension.

To silence gossip regarding yourself.

To gain the discernment to separate truth from lies.

12th House of the Subconscious, Dreams, and Secrets:

To end procrastination.

Words of Power

KAH-AH-MEE-AH

KAH-SHEF-EE-YEL

AH-MEE-YEL

MEN-EE-YEL

HAL-FAHS

39. MALPHAS

Planetary Aspect

Sun square/opposite Mercury

Applications in the 12 houses

1st House of Self:

To bring clarity and wisdom to avoid useless ego-driven arguments with others.

To bring flexibility regarding our ideas.

2nd House of Possessions:

To enable detailed and precise control over our finances and inventory of our possessions.

3rd House of Communications:

To avoid detours while traveling and arrive swiftly and safely at our destination.

To enable swift and clear communication.

4th House of Home:

To bring peace and resolution of disputes or disagreements between our parents and our self.

To bring harmony to our homelife.

5th House of Creativity:

To cause others to be silent when they disturb the peace.

To cause others to keep secrets.

6th House of Service and Health:

To bring organization, clarity, and confidence when one would be otherwise overwhelmed by one's workload.

7th House of Marriage and Partnership:

To reach satisfying agreement in debates or negotiations.

8th House of Death and New Beginnings

To make clear and rational decisions during stressful and confusing times.

9th House of Mental Exploration:

To see all sides of an argument with clarity before coming to a decision.

10th House of Career

To make a good impression on your superiors.

To speak clearly and confidently with those above your rank and cause them to give credence to your words.

11th House of Hopes, Wishes, and Friends

To understand the hidden agenda of others in regard to our self.

12th House of the Subconscious, Dreams, and Secrets

To ease worry and anxiety regarding our life's situations.

Words of Power

REH-HAW-EL

RAW-KEM-EE-YEL

HAH-KEE-ZEE-TAH-EL

AH-NEE-YEL

MAL-FAHS

40. RAUM

__Planetary Aspect__

Sun square/opposite Moon

__Applications in the 12 houses__

1st House of Self:

To express yourself with ease.

To ensure that what you say is what you mean.

To stay on course to achieve our goals.

2nd House of Possessions:

To bring aid to the management of our finances during times of financial trouble.

3rd House of Communications:

To overcome delays in progress towards our goals.

4th House of Home:

To bring peace and harmony to our home.

5th House of Creativity:

For wisdom regarding investment decisions.

6th House of Service and Health:

To bring strength to deal with hectic situations at work.

To cause harmony between coworkers.

7th House of Marriage and Partnership:

To encourage cooperation in our partnerships with others.

To encourage others to keep their agreements with us.

8th House of Death and New Beginnings:

To make wise financial decisions.

9th House of Mental Exploration:

To discover a path that leads to one's dreams becoming reality.

10th House of Career:

To maintain equilibrium during times of rapid change at one's place of work.

11th House of Hopes, Wishes, and Friends:

To encourage others to cooperate with us.

12th House of the Subconscious, Dreams, and Secrets:

To bring peace to unresolved issues.

Words of Power

YAY-EASE-EL

YAR-ETZ-EE-YEL

YEH-GAR-EH-TZEE-YEL

ZAH-KREE-YEL

RAWM

41. FORCALOR

__Planetary Aspect__

Venus square/opposite Neptune

__Applications in the 12 houses__

1st House of Self:

To see ourselves as we truly are.

To understand our true capabilities.

2nd House of Possessions:

To put our money towards a practical and beneficial use.

3rd House of Communications:

To understand the truth of what others, say to us.

To see others as they truly are.

4th House of Home:

To gain courage to reveal the truth of who one is to one's family.

5th House of Creativity:

To develop one's imagination to a high level.

To bring great creative inspiration.

6th House of Service and Health:

To understand the most profitable and enjoyable direction to take in one's career.

7th House of Marriage and Partnership:

To see a partner as they truly are, beyond lies and illusions.

8th House of Death and New Beginnings

To understand our true potential and how we may fulfill it.

9th House of Mental Exploration:

To understand the truth of a philosophy or teaching.

10th House of Career

To discover a fruitful and beneficial career path to take.

11th House of Hopes, Wishes, and Friends

To see the true value of a group or organization.

12th House of the Subconscious, Dreams, and Secrets

To silence harmful and self-destructive thoughts that hinder us.

Words of Power

HAH-AH-EL

HAHK-MEE-YEL

HAHT-ZAHF-EATS-EE-YEL

HAW-SHAH-EH-EE-YEL

FOUR-KAH-LOHR

42. VEPAR

Planetary Aspect

Venus square/opposite Saturn

Applications in the 12 houses

1st House of Self:

To reestablish lost connections with others.

2nd House of Possessions:

To save money.

3rd House of Communications:

To bring confidence to communication with others.

To bring social grace and eloquence.

4th House of Home:

To bring strength to fulfill obligations to one's family.

5th House of Creativity:

To bring fresh life to a relationship that has gone stale.

To bring enrich life so that we may enjoy it when life feels dull.

6th House of Service and Health:

To bring strength to endure hard work effectively.

To encourage our superiors to be more lenient.

7th House of Marriage and Partnership:

To bring trust to a relationship.

8th House of Death and New Beginnings:

To encourage others to lend us money.

9th House of Mental Exploration:

To remain strong and full of hope when one's faith in magick is tested.

10th House of Career:

To cause superiors to see the value of what we have to offer.

11th House of Hopes, Wishes, and Friends:

To bring harmony and confidence when faced with unavoidable awkward gatherings or situations.

12th House of the Subconscious, Dreams, and Secrets:

To swiftly resolve unfinished business.

To overcome procrastination.

Words of Power

MEE-KAH-EL

MAH-TED-EE-YEL

YAW-TEN-EE-YEL

KAH-DESH-EE-MAH-EL

VEH-PAR

43. SABNOCK

Planetary Aspect

Venus square/opposite Jupiter

Applications in the 12 houses

1st House of Self:

To bring discipline not to self-indulge.

2nd House of Possessions:

To be mindful and wise of how we use our money and resources.

To get the best value for investments of our time and energy.

3rd House of Communications:

To avoid being taken advantage of by others.

To act and speak according to our true will.

4th House of Home:

To create a peaceful period of rest and rejuvenation.

5th House of Creativity:

To find a new romantic relationship.

To ensure that both parties in a relationship understand the nature of the relationship and the expectations of their partner.

6th House of Service and Health:

To encourage others to contribute at work so that you aren't required to shoulder the full burden.

7th House of Marriage and Partnership:

To create harmony and peace in long term relationships.

8th House of Death and New Beginnings:

To overcome laziness and self-indulgence.

9th House of Mental Exploration:

To bring mutual understanding between those of different cultural backgrounds.

10th House of Career:

To bring general good luck to your career aspirations.

To be careful not to promise more than you can give.

11th House of Hopes, Wishes, and Friends:

To make connections with those who may help you achieve career success.

12th House of the Subconscious, Dreams, and Secrets:

To allow a period of rest with minimum side effects to your career

Words of Power

VEH-VAH-LEE-AH

VEN-AH-DEH-YEE-MAH-EL

VEN-AH-DEH-MEE-YEE-VAH-EL

LEH-KAH-KEM-EE-YEL

SAHB-NOCK

44. SHAX

Planetary Aspect

Venus square/opposite Mars

Applications in the 12 houses

1st House of Self:

To increase popularity with the opposite sex.

To increase the chances of a romantic encounter.

2nd House of Possessions:

To help one to stick to a budget.

To bring mutual understanding between two parties regarding finances or possessions.

3rd House of Communications:

To find a harmonious resolution to a conflict.

4th House of Home:

To bring peace to a domestic dispute.

5th House of Creativity:

To inspire a passionate romantic relationship to blossom.

To ensure both partners give and take equally in a relationship.

6th House of Service and Health:

To encourage cooperation with coworkers.

To ensure everyone bears the workload equally in our place of work.

7th House of Marriage and Partnership:

To ease jealousy in a long-term relationship.

To restore broken trust in a relationship.

8th House of Death and New Beginnings:

To encourage an attitude of giving and generosity in regard to financial agreements.

9th House of Mental Exploration:

To encourage swift resolution of a legal issue outside of the court system.

To encourage another to be more open to a change.

10th House of Career:

To be seen as an agreeable leader.

To obtain the support of one's subordinates.

The be unmoved by the jealousy of others regarding our success.

11th House of Hopes, Wishes, and Friends:

To encourage trust in our friends and associates.

To ensure those with whom we strike deals understand the terms of the agreement clearly.

12th House of the Subconscious, Dreams, and Secrets:

To understand the hidden meaning behind the words and actions of others towards us.

__Words of Power__

YEL-AH-EE-YAH

YAW-DEE-YEL

LAH-DAH-DEE-YEL

HA-HA-DEE-YEL

SHOCKS

45. VINE

Planetary Aspect

Venus square/opposite Sun

Applications in the 12 houses

1st House of Self:

To bring discipline to avoid overindulgence.

To turn our focus from our own needs to the needs and desires of others to gain their trust and respect.

2nd House of Possessions:

To perceive the true value of things.

To understand what we truly need and what can be discarded.

3rd House of Communications:

To establish clear boundaries so that others do not impose on us.

4th House of Home:

To establish privacy in our domestic life.

5th House of Creativity:

To be sure we thoroughly understand the value of an investment before we invest in it.

To keep away and silent those who disapprove of our taste in partners and encourage them to change their attitude.

6th House of Service and Health:

To develop a strong work ethic.

7th House of Marriage and Partnership:

To create a balance of power in a romantic or work relationship.

8th House of Death and New Beginnings

To foresee the consequences of an investment of our time or money to ensure the benefits are worth it.

9th House of Mental Exploration:

To cause those of different cultural, intellectual, or religious backgrounds to get along harmoniously and with mutual understanding.

10th House of Career

To overcome the jealousy of others and triumph over those who seek to hold us back.

To achieve a career promotion.

11th House of Hopes, Wishes, and Friends

To make a connection with those who can aid our goals in coming to fruition.

12th House of the Subconscious, Dreams, and Secrets

To focus in the midst of distractions that would otherwise cause you to procrastinate.

To increase your resolve to accomplish what you set out to do.

Words of Power

SEE-AH-LEE-AH

SAH-MEH-KEY-EL

AH-SEK-EE-YEL

LAH-KEH-SEE-YEL

VEE-NEH

46. BIFRONS

Planetary Aspect

Venus square/opposite Venus

Applications in the 12 houses

1st House of Self:

To encourage moderation in social situations to avoid offending others.

2nd House of Possessions:

To put the brakes on spending and understand how to best save money.

3rd House of Communications:

To create balance and harmony in your relationships with others.

4th House of Home:

To ensure that you are motivated to keep your place of living tidy and well organized.

5th House of Creativity:

To ensure both partners have enough space to breathe in a romantic relationship.

6th House of Service and Health:

To ensure that everyone bears the workload equally.

7th House of Marriage and Partnership:

To achieve a balance of intimacy, space, and understanding in a long-term relationship to ensure that both partners feel at ease.

8th House of Death and New Beginnings:

To increase one's ambition to achieve goals.

9th House of Mental Exploration:

To discover and focus on the similarities with have with others rather than our differences to create social harmony.

10th House of Career:

To create a balance of power and mutual understanding between leaders and their subordinates.

11th House of Hopes, Wishes, and Friends:

To see clearly who supports us and whose intentions and desires are different than our own.

The perceive those who seek to undermine our plans.

12th House of the Subconscious, Dreams, and Secrets:

To encourage those who feel helpless and weak to feel courageous, strong, and motivated.

Words of Power

ARE-EE-EL

AW-VEE-YEL

RAH-KEV-EE-YEH-VAH-EL

YAH-DEH-VAR-GAH-EL

BIH-FRAWNS

47. VUALL

__Planetary Aspect__

Venus square/opposite Mercury

__Applications in the 12 houses__

1st House of Self:

To cause others to spill secrets unintentionally through conversation.

2nd House of Possessions:

To understand the true value of our possessions.

To ensure one's finances are balanced and in order.

3rd House of Communications:

To maintain an equal balance of give and take in relationships.

To perceive the true reason that a person has sought you out.

4th House of Home:

To gain perspective of a situation that affects you.

5th House of Creativity:

To encourage love to be reciprocated.

To perceive a love interest as they truly are.

6th House of Service and Health:

To bring focus and productivity to your behavior at work.

7th House of Marriage and Partnership:

To gain insight into the true needs and desires of others.

To cause both parties to feel equally satisfied with a deal, transaction, or a trade.

8th House of Death and New Beginnings

To ensure that we live within our means and do not overspend.

9th House of Mental Exploration:

To ensure that you are not misrepresented.

To ensure you remain safe and supported when there is a conflict of interest.

10th House of Career

To see clearly when someone is trying to use or manipulate us for their own benefit.

11th House of Hopes, Wishes, and Friends

To perceive who has our best interest in mind and who would be harmful for us to befriend.

12th House of the Subconscious, Dreams, and Secrets

To ensure that we are punctual to appointments and our life runs smoothly and orderly.

To bring order to one's life through the discipline of creating a schedule.

Words of Power

ESH-AH-LEE-AH

AH-MEH-DEE-YEL

SHAH-MEH-SHE-YEL

LEE-YEL

VOO-AHL

48. HAAGENTI

Planetary Aspect

Venus square/opposite Moon

Applications in the 12 houses:

1st House of Self:

To remain focused and disciplined.

2nd House of Possessions:

To bring aid to saving money and avoid overspending.

3rd House of Communications:

To bring popularity with women.

To keep those at bay who seek to leech off of your generosity and kindness.

4th House of Home:

To stay on top of your work to ensure you do not fall behind.

5th House of Creativity:

To cause a romantic relationship to be fulfilling to both partners.

To create space in a relationship for each partner to be relaxed and have room to breathe and be.

6th House of Service and Health:

To cause coworkers to work in harmony, each shouldering the workload equally.

7th House of Marriage and Partnership:

To bring a peace, harmony, and balance to a marriage or long-term relationship.

8th House of Death and New Beginnings:

To encourage willpower, drive, and self-discipline.

9th House of Mental Exploration:

To bring mutual understanding and respect between people when there are significant differences between their cultural, spiritual, or intellectual outlooks.

10th House of Career:

To ensure that the truth of who you are is well presented and understood by all.

11th House of Hopes, Wishes, and Friends:

To ensure that our generosity is equally compensated.

12th House of the Subconscious, Dreams, and Secrets:

To create a space to rest, relax, and recuperate from a hectic time.

To ensure we reward our self and care for our needs.

Words of Power

MEE-HUH-EL

MAH-MEH-LEE-EL

YEH-KAH-LESH-EE-YAH-VEL

HAH-AH-ZEE-YEL

HAH-AH-GEN-TEE

49. CROCEL

Planetary Aspect

Mercury square/opposite Neptune

Applications in the 12 houses

1st House of Self:

To ensure one's perceptions are sharp and able to discern truth from fiction.

2nd House of Possessions:

To avoid mistakes in accounting and managing one's budget. To clearly see and understand the inflow and outflow of money in one's accounts.

3rd House of Communications:

To ensure one's messages are fully understood and well received.

4th House of Home:

To create harmony and peace in the home through mutual understanding.

5th House of Creativity:

To bring great creativity and innovation to one's artistic pursuits.

6th House of Service and Health:

To be sure that one's work is accurate, thorough, and complete.

7th House of Marriage and Partnership:

To avoid miscommunications between partners and ensure each person is well understood.

8th House of Death and New Beginnings:

To perceive one's true needs to enable personal transformation.

9th House of Mental Exploration:

To bring deep understanding of magick and occult philosophy.

10th House of Career:

To perceive with clarity the past career path to take.

11th House of Hopes, Wishes, and Friends:

To ensure discussions and debates take place harmoniously with mutual understanding and respect.

12th House of the Subconscious, Dreams, and Secrets:

To gain a deeper understanding of oneself through fruitful periods of meditation.

Words of Power

VEH-HOO-EL

VEH-OH-LEE-YEL

HAW-KEH-ZEE-YEL

VAH-GEH-REE-YEL

CROW-KEL

50. FURCAS

Planetary Aspect

Mercury square/opposite Saturn

Applications in the 12 houses

1st House of Self:

To gain a wide perspective regarding the truth of a situation.

2nd House of Possessions:

To develop the willpower to turn one's financial situation around from hopeless to hopeful.

3rd House of Communications:

To ensure one does not miss opportunities.

To bring relief from depression.

To aid sociability and allow one to communicate with ease.

4th House of Home:

To bring understanding to discussions with one's parents or other family members.

5th House of Creativity:

To bring harmony and healing to a relationship.

6th House of Service and Health:

To enable productivity and focus in one's work.

7th House of Marriage and Partnership:

To bring resolution to deep seated or long-term issues in a committed relationship.

8th House of Death and New Beginnings:

To transform pessimism to optimism.

9th House of Mental Exploration:

To bring breakthroughs in understanding of a teaching, science, or philosophy.

10th House of Career:

To enable one to successfully plan for a promotion or a change in careers.

To encourage superiors to be supportive.

11th House of Hopes, Wishes, and Friends:

To bring companionship when one feels alone or isolated.

12th House of the Subconscious, Dreams, and Secrets:

To ease depression and bring understanding of one's current situation in life.

Words of Power

DAH-NEE-EL

DAW-SEH-VEE-YEL

NAH-SEE-SEE-YEL

YAW-FEE-SEE-YEL

FUR-KAHS

51. BALAM

Planetary Aspect

Mercury square/opposite Jupiter

Applications in the 12 houses

1st House of Self:

To ensure one is perceiving reality as it truly is.

2nd House of Possessions:

To ensure one's finances and accounting is in order.

3rd House of Communications:

To bring success in studies at school.

4th House of Home:

To clearly understand the terms of a contract especially if the contract regards buying or selling a home.

5th House of Creativity:

To gain a full understanding of a situation to enable one to take the most appropriate actions.

6th House of Service and Health:

The keep the pace and stay on top of one's duties at work when things become busy or hectic.

7th House of Marriage and Partnership:

To bring mutual understanding to discussions between partners in a long-term relationship.

8th House of Death and New Beginnings:

To gain wisdom of one's life that bring transformation.

9th House of Mental Exploration:

To become a published author.

To maintain humility.

To be successful in one's college studies.

10th House of Career:

To understand clearly how one's career ambitions may best proceed.

11th House of Hopes, Wishes, and Friends:

To encourage a friendly and harmonious atmosphere in groups of which one is a part.

12th House of the Subconscious, Dreams, and Secrets:

To uncover secrets.

Words of Power

HAH-KAH-SHE-YAH

HAT-ZEET-EE-VAH-EL

KAHTZ-ET-AH-EL

SHEF-TEHT-ZAH-EL

BAH-LAHM

52. ALLOCES

Planetary Aspect

Mercury square/opposite Mars

Applications in the 12 houses

1st House of Self:

To bring peace to arguments.

To bring calm when tempers flare.

2nd House of Possessions:

To make only premeditated actions regarding financial matters to avoid making mistakes that could have been prevented.

3rd House of Communications:

To bring safety while driving.

4th House of Home:

To bring peace and harmony to one's home.

5th House of Creativity:

To find a creative outlet for one's frustrations and anger that is peaceful and beneficial.

6th House of Service and Health:

To bring strength and discipline to accomplish a great deal of work.

7th House of Marriage and Partnership:

To bring peace to arguments in a long-term relationship or marriage.

8th House of Death and New Beginnings:

To bring harmony to our finances.

To ease financial fears and stress.

9th House of Mental Exploration:

To bring mutual understanding and peace to tense discussions and debates.

10th House of Career:

To protect your reputation.

11th House of Hopes, Wishes, and Friends:

To cause a debate to be mutually beneficial for all involved.

12th House of the Subconscious, Dreams, and Secrets:

To calm anxiety or mental agitation.

Words of Power

AW-MEM-EE-AH

AH-SHEH-FEE-EL

MAH-SHEH-TEE-YEL

MEH-KAH-RET-ZEE-EL

AH-LOH-KEYZ

53. CAIM

Planetary Aspect

Mercury square/opposite Sun

Applications in the 12 houses

1st House of Self:

To bring understanding of others.

2nd House of Possessions:

To be aware of our finances and keep them in order.

To avoid overspending.

3rd House of Communications:

To understand the true needs of those we communicate with and so avoid arguments.

4th House of Home:

To bring harmony to one's personal life.

To bring clear communication and mutual understanding to discussions with parents.

5th House of Creativity:

To express oneself clearly and concisely.

6th House of Service and Health:

To bring competence to complete tasks when a deadline is approaching at work.

7th House of Marriage and Partnership:

To portray ourselves exactly as we wish to be portrayed so that we are understood by others.

8th House of Death and New Beginnings

To encourage secrets to remain hidden.

To know who is trustworthy and who is not.

9th House of Mental Exploration:

To bring a swift, safe, and productive travel experience.

10th House of Career

To understand the desires of superiors and how to get on their good side for our benefit.

11th House of Hopes, Wishes, and Friends

To bring harmony and cooperation in a group so that all are on one accord and working towards a single goal.

12th House of the Subconscious, Dreams, and Secrets

To ease headaches.

To enable one to relax fully.

To make plans effectively and with clarity.

Words of Power

NEN-AH-EL

NEH-SAH-TEH-FEE-EL

NEH-SEE-EL

AH-VEH-REE-YEL

CAH-MEE-OH

54. MURMUS

Planetary Aspect

Mercury square/opposite Venus

Applications in the 12 houses

1st House of Self:

To have the willpower to remain concentrated on a desired task.

2nd House of Possessions:

To protect from losses due to negligence.

3rd House of Communications:

To stand one's ground when others make unreasonable demands.

4th House of Home:

To bring the confidence to have a difficult conversation with relatives.

5th House of Creativity:

To bring understand the art of charm and how to use it to encourage romantic interests to reciprocate your attraction to them.

6th House of Service and Health:

To keep secrets and rumors from spreading at work.

To discover secrets and rumors others seek to hide from you.

To be disciplined and focused at work.

7th House of Marriage and Partnership:

To reach a mutual understanding regarding long held or undiscussed issues with another.

8th House of Death and New Beginnings

To breakthrough to new levels of wisdom and understanding in our life to achieve success in a desired goal.

9th House of Mental Exploration:

To bring protection while traveling and cause travels to go smoothly.

To cause tense negotiations to go smoothly.

10th House of Career

To bring confidence when meeting with one who is higher status or position than you.

11th House of Hopes, Wishes, and Friends

To gain popularity in a desired circle.

12th House of the Subconscious, Dreams, and Secrets

To discover things others, try to keep hidden.

Words of Power

NEE-TUH-EL

NAHTZ-BEE-YEL

YAH-AHT-ZEE-YEL

TAH-TEHT-ZEE-YEL

MER-MUSS

55. OROBAS

Planetary Aspect

Mercury square/opposite Mercury

Applications in the 12 houses

1st House of Self:

To bring peace and a sense of ease during hectic times.

To express oneself eloquently.

2nd House of Possessions:

To keep one's finances under control and in order.

3rd House of Communications:

To accomplish tasks and errands swiftly and without distraction or delay.

4th House of Home:

To bring peace during worrisome times.

5th House of Creativity:

To cause all whom you encounter to see you as likeable.

To have a disposition that brings the admiration and respect of others.

6th House of Service and Health:

To accomplish one's tasks with accuracy.

7th House of Marriage and Partnership:

To communicate clearly and effectively with others.

8th House of Death and New Beginnings:

To bring mental clarity and understanding on an issue of import.

9th House of Mental Exploration:

To guard possessions against being lost or stolen.

10th House of Career:

To bring confidence and dignity when speaking before the public.

To cause others too think highly of you.

11th House of Hopes, Wishes, and Friends:

To bring a fruitful exchange of ideas between others.

To cause a group to be organized.

12th House of the Subconscious, Dreams, and Secrets:

To ensure that your message is heard and well understood.

To ease feelings of panic or anxiety.

Words of Power

MEE-VAH-EE-AH

MAH-KEE-YEL

VAW-EL

HAH-REH-EE-YEL

OH-ROH-BAHS

56. GREMORI

Planetary Aspect

Mercury square/opposite Moon

Applications in the 12 houses

1st House of Self:

To perceive others clearly and without deception.

To bring out the best in oneself and others.

2nd House of Possessions:

To bring order to your financial life in regard to budgeting.

To transform your financial life in accordance with your will (this implies it requires you to put in work and effort to transform it, Gremori will guide you).

3rd House of Communications:

To cause conversation with others to flow easily and enjoyably.

To minimize small daily inconveniences.

4th House of Home:

To bring harmony and peace to one's home during times of chaos or upheaval.

5th House of Creativity:

To express yourself harmoniously so that others appreciate your words and find you amiable.

6th House of Service and Health:

To bring smooth and harmonious cooperation with our co-workers.

7th House of Marriage and Partnership:

To bring mutual understanding to a relationship or partnership when disagreements abound.

8th House of Death and New Beginnings:

To inspire positive thinking that allows you to transform your current troublesome circumstances into beneficial ones.

9th House of Mental Exploration:

To perceive the truth of any situation with clarity to enable you to make a wise decision.

To uncover hidden secrets that can transform your life in a positive manner if acted upon.

10th House of Career:

To gain insight into what the most profitable and enjoyable career path would be for you.

To understand a group and how to gain popularity in it.

11th House of Hopes, Wishes, and Friends:

To cause others to cooperate with you and support you.

12th House of the Subconscious, Dreams, and Secrets:

To lighten the mood of yourself or others during times of tension.

<u>Words of Power</u>

PAW-EE-EL

PAH-NAH-EL

VAHT-ZEH-LEE-YEE-EL

YAW-DEH-SHAH-DEE-YEL

GREM-OAR-EE

57. OSE

Planetary Aspect

Moon square/opposite Neptune

Applications in the 12 houses

1st House of Self:

To bring the courage to face the world head on.

To become grounded and focused.

2nd House of Possessions:

To gain a clear insight into one's financial situation and transform it at will.

3rd House of Communications:

To enable beneficial and accurate decisions to be made during negotiations with others.

To understand the underlying message beneath someone's words and actions.

4th House of Home:

To clear the atmosphere of strange and awkward moods and restore normalcy.

5th House of Creativity:

To inspire great creative inspiration.

To think of new and innovated ideas.

6th House of Service and Health:

To discover ways of working more efficiently and productively.

7th House of Marriage and Partnership:

To ensure that you see eye to eye with your partner.

8th House of Death and New Beginnings:

To envision clearly what you desire to become and make that vision a reality.

To transform the mind and emotions of others as will.

9th House of Mental Exploration:

To understand magick and occult philosophy on a deep level.

To discover the source of all magick and power.

10th House of Career:

To achieve a desired career promotion.

To be appear agreeable to those who can make your desires become true.

11th House of Hopes, Wishes, and Friends:

To perceive one's true desires and understand the path to fulfill those desires.

12th House of the Subconscious, Dreams, and Secrets:

To cause another to believe what you wish them to.

To change subconscious beliefs to transform your life.

Words of Power

NEM-EM-EE-AH

NOO-REE-YEL

MAH-EH-SHAH-NEE-YEL

MAW-KET-EE-YEL

OH-SEH

58. AMY

Planetary Aspect

Moon square/opposite Saturn

Applications in the 12 houses

1st House of Self:

To bring confidence to express your emotions truthfully.

To be self-sufficient.

2nd House of Possessions:

To encourage others to lend generously to you.

3rd House of Communications:

To care for others who rely on you.

4th House of Home:

To encourage your family or close relatives to be supportive of you.

5th House of Creativity:

To gain the confidence to express your love for someone.

6th House of Service and Health:

To create a supportive environment of mutual help in the workplace.

7th House of Marriage and Partnership:

To encourage those, we are in partnership with to fulfill what we require of them.

8th House of Death and New Beginnings:

To raise one's thoughts to higher and more positive things when one is depressed.

To ease your mind when your thoughts seem to dwell on death and human mortality.

9th House of Mental Exploration:

To maintain an attitude of hope and positivity.

10th House of Career:

To bring the strength to deal with responsibilities in our career.

11th House of Hopes, Wishes, and Friends:

To interact with groups you are a part of in harmony.

To ensure all within a group have a feeling of belonging.

12th House of the Subconscious, Dreams, and Secrets:

To ease depression through friendship.

To find a true friend when going through a period of loneliness.

Words of Power

YEH-YEE-LUH-EL

YEH-ROO-SHE-YEL

YEET-ZEH-TOO-VAH-EL

LAH-GEH-BEE-YEL

AH-MEE

59. ORIAS

Planetary Aspect

Moon square/opposite Jupiter

Applications in the 12 houses

1st House of Self:

To bring the quality of moderation and control to one's personality.

2nd House of Possessions:

To maintain your budget and prevent overspending.

3rd House of Communications:

To establish clear boundaries with interpersonal relationship.

4th House of Home:

To bring relief when relatives claim too much of your time.

5th House of Creativity:

To create space for both partners in a relationship when feeling stifled.

6th House of Service and Health:

To improve one's mood in the workplace.

To ease feelings of depression.

7th House of Marriage and Partnership:

To brighten the mood of a relationship after a fight and restore harmony and mutual respect.

8th House of Death and New Beginnings:

To perceive one's true needs beyond the illusion of the mind.

9th House of Mental Exploration:

To ensure your intentions are well understood by others. Cause others to respect you and hold you in high regard.

10th House of Career:

To achieve a career promotion.

To show employers to see you as strong and capable.

11th House of Hopes, Wishes, and Friends:

To cause groups you are a part of to cooperate and have an attitude of respect for each other.

To clear the air in a group of people when the mood turns sour.

12th House of the Subconscious, Dreams, and Secrets:

To strengthen ones focus on the present when there is a tendency to daydream.

Words of Power

HAH-RAH-KEL

HAH-REH-KEY-VAH-EL

RAH-KEH-KEY-YEL

KAH-KEH-MEE-YEL

OAR-EE-AHS

60. VAPULA

Planetary Aspect

Moon square/opposite Mars

Applications in the 12 houses

1st House of Self:

To ease an irritable mood.

To see a situation objectively.

2nd House of Possessions:

To ease worries regarding one's finances.

3rd House of Communications:

To bring protection while traveling.

To bring the strength to deal with troublesome people and conversations.

4th House of Home:

To create harmony and peace in a family.

5th House of Creativity:

To put an end to arguments.

6th House of Service and Health:

To bring calm to a stressful situation or time at work.

7th House of Marriage and Partnership:

To ease tension in a relationship.

To calm a tendency to fight in long term relationship and partnerships.

8th House of Death and New Beginnings:

To ease worry regarding one's financial situation.

9th House of Mental Exploration:

To bring the strength to deal with overbearing people.

10th House of Career:

To develop great skill in one's job.

To develop the talents necessary to for a career change.

To fulfill career ambitions.

11th House of Hopes, Wishes, and Friends:

To quell anger in a group.

To ease political tension.

12th House of the Subconscious, Dreams, and Secrets

To ease tension, anger, and stress in oneself.

Words of Power

MET-ZEH-REL

MAH-TEM-EE-YEL

TZOO-REE-YEL

RAW-SHE-YEL

VAH-POO-LAH

61. ZAGAN

Planetary Aspect

Moon square/opposite Sun

Applications in the 12 houses

1st House of Self:

To bring unite the conscious and unconscious selves to bring inner harmony and decisiveness.

2nd House of Possessions:

To bring harmony to one's financial affairs and maintain a budget.

3rd House of Communications:

To balance our needs with the needs of others to create harmony.

4th House of Home:

To end arguments between one's parents.

To find work-life balance.

5th House of Creativity:

To eloquently express oneself.

To discover satisfaction in one's love life.

6th House of Service and Health:

To be capable during times of chaos and stress in the work-place.

7th House of Marriage and Partnership:

To bring harmony and understanding between partners regarding the direction the relationship is heading.

To understand the needs of your partner in love or business.

8th House of Death and New Beginnings:

To bring financial support from others.

9th House of Mental Exploration:

To find stability and remain grounded and centered when undergoing an existential crisis or a paradigm shift.

10th House of Career:

To bring harmony to a relationship with your superiors at work.

To have a fulfilling career while also enjoying one's personal life fully.

11th House of Hopes, Wishes, and Friends:

To get along well with friends.

To cause a group to operate on one accord.

12th House of the Subconscious, Dreams, and Secrets:

To resolve unfinished business.

To bring a project to completion.

Words of Power

OO-MAH-BEL

VAH-ED-EE-YEL

MAHT-ZEFF-EE-VAH-EL

BAR-ECK-EE-YEL

ZAH-GAHN

62. VALAC

Planetary Aspect

Moon square/opposite Venus

Applications in the 12 houses

1st House of Self:

To ease feelings of possessiveness or jealousy in self or others.

2nd House of Possessions:

To curb impulsiveness.

To make wise financial decisions.

3rd House of Communications:

To fulfil one's obligations to friends and family.

4th House of Home:

To bring space to accomplish personal goals when others demand your time and attention.

5th House of Creativity:

To make your love felt by a romantic partner to calm feelings of possessiveness or jealousy in them.

6th House of Service and Health:

To create healthy boundaries and space between coworkers and oneself.

To bring strength and discipline to work hard and not be lazy.

To end procrastination.

7th House of Marriage and Partnership:

To discover and resolve the underlying reason behind a partner's manipulative or jealous behavior.

8th House of Death and New Beginnings:

To curb a tendency to overspend or live beyond ones means.

9th House of Mental Exploration:

To bring harmony between opposites.

To bring understanding when there are vast differences culturally or ideologically.

10th House of Career:

To bring relief when the burden of responsibilities at a job weighs heavy on us (may take the form of additional breaks or others shouldering the load).

11th House of Hopes, Wishes, and Friends:

To develop the skill of holding the attention of others through fascinating conversational ability.

To become popular in a group.

12th House of the Subconscious, Dreams, and Secrets:

To develop wisdom regarding any subject of import.

Words of Power

YAH-AH-EL

YAW-VEH-FEE-YEL

HAW-SHET-EH-MEE-YEL

HAH-LEE-YEE-VAH-EL

Tristan Whitespire

VAH-AHK

63. ANDRAS

Planetary Aspect

Moon square/opposite Mercury

Applications in the 12 houses

1st House of Self:

To bring inner peace when your thoughts are in conflict with your feelings.

To make the right decision when blinded by emotions.

2nd House of Possessions:

To put a stop to impulsive spending.

3rd House of Communications:

To bring resolution when one has been offended or offended another in a relationship.

4th House of Home:

To bring peace, calm, and order to one's home.

5th House of Creativity:

To resolve misunderstandings.

To express yourself clearly to avoid misunderstandings

through miscommunication.

6th House of Service and Health:

To resolve chaos in one's workplace.

7th House of Marriage and Partnership:

To remain calm when one intentionally tries to anger you.

To bring calm, clear, and rational discussion in a relationship to enable mutual understanding.

8th House of Death and New Beginnings:

To ease dark or depressing thoughts.

To ease worry.

9th House of Mental Exploration:

To find relief from nightmares or night terrors and sleep peacefully.

To feel safe and secure.

10th House of Career:

To enable clear minded and objective thought when making decisions regarding your career.

11th House of Hopes, Wishes, and Friends:

To see others as they really are so you know what to expect of them.

12th House of the Subconscious, Dreams, and Secrets:

To be focused when there is a tendency to daydream.

Words of Power

AH-NOO-EL

AH-TEH-TZAH-ME-YEL

NAH-TEH-KEY-EL

VAH-ET-OO-ME-YEL

AND-RASS

64. HAURES

Planetary Aspect

Moon square/opposite Moon

Applications in the 12 houses

1st House of Self:

To end self-abuse and self-hatred.

To understand your feelings.

2nd House of Possessions:

To bring peace to arguments regarding finances or possessions.

3rd House of Communications:

To bring rationality to all parties involved in a dispute.

4th House of Home:

To cause one's homelife to flow smoothly and orderly.

5th House of Creativity:

To bring peace to upset regarding one's romantic life.

6th House of Service and Health:

To bring work-life balance.

7th House of Marriage and Partnership:

To bring an attitude of mutual support, understanding, and harmony between partners.

8th House of Death and New Beginnings:

To bring peace to the issue of finances to prevent disputes.

9th House of Mental Exploration:

To remain hopeful when the situation looks grim.

10th House of Career:

To cause superiors and coworkers to hold your ideas in high esteem.

To be recognized for innovative thinking on the job.

11th House of Hopes, Wishes, and Friends:

To bring the strength to work independently.

To cause others to support you when you feel overwhelmed.

12th House of the Subconscious, Dreams, and Secrets:

To perceive the cause of upset or unbalance clearly within oneself to resolve it.

Words of Power

MAH-KEY-EL

MAH-LEH-KEY-EE-EL

KAH-SHAF-EE-SHE-YEL

YEH-HEE-YEL

HOR-EZ

Note: The following eight spirits represents the qualities and attributes on their respective planets grounded and expressed on Earth in action. These spirits embody the attributes of their respective planets. For example, Belial is known to be powerful, aggressive, and very direct. This is because he represents Mars embodied on Earth.

Seer on the other hand is known to be amiable, fast acting, pleasant, very courteous and willing. This is because he represents the qualities and attributes of Venus embodied on earth.

Dantalion is known to be a master of the mind, manipulating thoughts and minds at will, etc. This is because he represents the qualities and attributes of Mercury embodied on earth.

65. ANDREALPHUS

Planetary Aspect

Neptune on Earth

Applications in the 12 houses

1st House of Self:

To bring inspiration when feeling dull or uninspired.

To see oneself with clarity.

2nd House of Possessions:

To reveal one's potential for gain in any situation.

To show the true value of things.

3rd House of Communications:

To encourage stimulating, enriching conversations with others.

4th House of Home:

To design one's home is accordance with personal aesthetics.

5th House of Creativity:

To bring creative inspiration so one may produce innovative works of art.

6th House of Service and Health:

To restore beauty and mystery to mundane life.

7th House of Marriage and Partnership:

To bring back a feeling excitement to revitalize a dull relationship.

8th House of Death and New Beginnings:

To become that which we desire to become.

9th House of Mental Exploration:

To understand high philosophy and occult knowledge in a grounded way so that we can apply it to achieve practical results.

10th House of Career:

To discover a career path that brings us joy and feels right for us.

11th House of Hopes, Wishes, and Friends:

To bring harmony to groups.

12th House of the Subconscious, Dreams, and Secrets:

To understand how to bring our dreams into reality.

To gain a sense of the future.

Words of Power

DAH-MEH-BEE-AH

DAW-DEN-EE-YEL

MAH-SHEF-EE-DAH-EL

BEE-VAH-EL

AHN-DREH-AHL-FUS

66. CIMERIES

Planetary Aspect

Saturn on Earth

Applications in the 12 houses

1st House of Self:

To express oneself clearly.

To develop discipline and tenacity.

2nd House of Possessions:

To discover hidden talents and abilities.

To discover value in things we have overlooked.

To discover pathways that lead to wealth.

3rd House of Communications:

To cause others to reveal secrets in conversation.

To cause a difficult or tense conversation to be fruitful and productive.

To cause another to be silent.

4th House of Home:

To make another see reason when they are irrational.

5th House of Creativity:

To influence the thoughts of another to bend to your will through conversation.

6th House of Service and Health:

To make a superior at work heed your words.

7th House of Marriage and Partnership:

To bring back a partner who has strayed.

To enable clear and relational discussion between partners to resolve differences.

8th House of Death and New Beginnings:

To understand what you truly desire and bring wisdom to achieve it.

9th House of Mental Exploration:

To understand difficult philosophies.

To cause others to see the error of their ways.

10th House of Career:

To maintain your career when it is threatened.

11th House of Hopes, Wishes, and Friends:

To influence a group to see things from your perspective.

12th House of the Subconscious, Dreams, and Secrets:

To bring order to unconscious impulses that sabotage you.

Words of Power

MEN-AH-KEL

MEH-KEY-YEL

NAH-TEH-REE-YEL

KEH-DAW-SHE-YEL

KIM-AIR-EASE

67. AMDUCIAS

Jupiter on Earth

Applications in the 12 houses

1st House of Self:

To inspire a good mood in self or others.

To be optimistic.

2nd House of Possessions:

To bring good luck in all things.

To bring money unexpectedly and in a pleasant manner.

To bring good fortune to acquiring new possessions.

3rd House of Communications:

To make others amiable in conversation.

To encourage others to cooperate with you.

To share or receive wisdom.

4th House of Home:

To create an atmosphere of peace and positivity in the home.

5th House of Creativity:

To inspire creative ideas that may be financially profitable.

To become popular for what you create.

6th House of Service and Health:

To accomplish a great deal of work without too much strain (you still must work hard but Amducias works to minimize feelings of strain).

To achieve fitness goals such as losing weight or gaining muscle.

7th House of Marriage and Partnership:

To cause a partner to remain loyal to you.

To cause a partner to be agreeable and good natured towards you.

8th House of Death and New Beginnings:

To become genuinely optimistic.

To ease depression.

9th House of Mental Exploration:

For success in one's studies.

To do well on tests.

To bring honors, accolades, and rewards.

10th House of Career:

To obtain promotion.

To discover a career path that brings wealth.

11th House of Hopes, Wishes, and Friends:

To cause a group to hold you in high esteem.

12th House of the Subconscious, Dreams, and Secrets:

To reveal one's flaws and negative character traits clearly so that we can resolve them and become a better person.

Words of Power

EE-AH-EL

AWE-REN-EE-YEL

YOO-REE-EL

AH-REH-TAH-SHE-EL

AHM-DO-KEY-AHS

68. BELIAL

Planetary Aspect

Mars on Earth

Applications in the 12 houses

1st House of Self:

To become confident, assertive, and full of courage.

To gain strength to overcome any obstacle.

2nd House of Possessions:

To increase one's income.

To protect one's possessions and valuables.

3rd House of Communications:

To win debates, disputes and arguments.

To silence all opposition.

4th House of Home:

To gain the respect of family, that they see you as a leader.

5th House of Creativity:

To reach new levels of creative skill that were before unattainable.

6th House of Service and Health:

To be seen as strong and capable at work.

To regain robust energy when feeling weak, tired, and down-trodden.

7th House of Marriage and Partnership:

To create passionate sexual desire in a partner.

To dominate a relationship and cause your partner to submit to you.

8th House of Death and New Beginnings:

To attract a partner for casual sex.

To bring the strength to attain a desired personal goal.

To end bad habits.

9th House of Mental Exploration:

For mental domination of self or others so that one's desires are fulfilled.

10th House of Career:

To attain a promotion to a high level of leadership.

To develop a reputation of power in one's career.

11th House of Hopes, Wishes, and Friends:

To achieve respect and recognition from a group.

12th House of the Subconscious, Dreams, and Secrets:

To control destructive subconscious impulses.

To master oneself through discipline.

Words of Power

KAH-VOO-EE-AH

KAH-MAH-KEH-ME-YEL

BAH-REK-EE-EL

VEN-ACK-TEE-YEL

BELL-EE-YEL

69. DECARABIA

Planetary Aspect

Sun on Earth

Applications in the 12 houses

1st House of Self:

To bring courage and self-esteem.

2nd House of Possessions:

To bring financial abundance.

3rd House of Communications:

To communicate with authority.

4th House of Home:

To cause the respect of one's family.

5th House of Creativity:

To inspire a period of prodigious creativity.

To achieve honor and respect for one's creative output.

6th House of Service and Health:

To encourage good health of mind and body.

To shine in the workplace.

7th House of Marriage and Partnership:

Brings harmony to a relationship.

8th House of Death and New Beginnings:

To give the energy to see what needs to be changed in one's personality and change it.

To encourage others to shower us with blessings and acts of goodwill.

9th House of Mental Exploration:

To bring illumination and enlightenment regarding difficult or complex studies.

10th House of Career:

To reach the pinnacle of success in one's career.

To be held in high esteem.

11th House of Hopes, Wishes, and Friends:

To gain the respect and admiration of others.

12th House of the Subconscious, Dreams, and Secrets:

To gain penetrating insight into those qualities in our self that hinder our success and change them at will.

Words of Power

RAH-AH-EL

REH-HOO-YAH-EL

AW-OO-MEH-LAH-NEE-YEL

HAH-KEH-TAH-KEE-YEL

DECK-AH-RAH-BEE-YAH

70. SEER

Planetary Aspect

Venus on Earth

Applications in the 12 houses

1st House of Self:

To create changes in our appearance (through natural means, exercise etc..) or personality at will and swiftly.

To change the way others perceive us.

2nd House of Possessions:

To bring a desired sum of money (much like the spirit Nitika, he brings moderate amounts quickly).

To discover a pathway to wealth.

To acquire material objects. (a new house, car, etc. May be very quickly by miraculous means but often they come naturally, in stages, but more quickly than otherwise thought possible.)

3rd House of Communications:

To communicate with those whom we have been long out of touch with.

To ensure our message is heard and understood by those with whom we speak.

To bring understanding of a difficult subject or situation so that we act in the most appropriate way (this can help with school studies or difficult social situations to restore harmony).

4th House of Home:

To bring aid to our parents when they are in need of help.

To protect one's home from theft and return stolen or borrowed items quickly.

To find lost items.

5th House of Creativity:

To find a new lover.

To recover the simple, quiet joy of life and living.

To receive fresh ideas and creative inspiration.

6th House of Service and Health:

To bring success to any project at work.

To ensure coworkers work harmoniously.

To enable prodigious productivity at work.

7th House of Marriage and Partnership:

To create harmony in a romantic relationship or business partnership.

To help others who are in need of assistance when we aren't sure how best to help them.

8th House of Death and New Beginnings

To transform your mind or personality to create the life you desire.

To bring money from afar (may receive unexpected money, money from a relative, refunds, prize winnings, etc.)

To restore and resurrect oneself when feeling down and out and defeated.

9th House of Mental Exploration:

To bring understanding and wisdom regarding any matter of import.

To develop great skill in magick.

To develop psychic abilities.

10th House of Career:

To achieve a promotion.

To be well liked by superiors.

To fulfill ambitions in life.

11th House of Hopes, Wishes, and Friends:

To merge with a group and be accepted.

To achieve fame.

To gain entrance into places that would otherwise be closed to you (could be a society, a physical location, or even the someone's heart).

12th House of the Subconscious, Dreams, and Secrets:

To learn secrets.

To perceive the hidden agenda of another.

To establish communication with the subconscious to plant messages which blossom into life transformation.

__Words of Power__

YAH-BAH-MEE-YAH

YAH-NEH-KEY-YEL

BAH-REH-KEE-YEL

MAH-LEH-KEY-YEL

SEE-AH

71. DANTALION

Planetary Aspect

Mercury on Earth

Applications in the 12 houses

1st House of Self:

To take on the mannerisms and attributes of whom one desires (not likely to change appearance but it is possible to create the illusion of a changed appearance).

To transform self-perception to achieve confidence and success.

To transform one's outlook on any person, subject, or life itself to overcome negativity.

2nd House of Possessions:

To acquire money and gifts from others through charm or deception.

3rd House of Communications:

To change the mind of another and influence their behavior to your benefit.

To become a charming conversationalist.

To bring necessary information from afar to further one's goals.

4th House of Home:

To bring clear and harmonious conversation with our family.

To heal rifts between family members and bring reconciliation.

5th House of Creativity:

To gain skill in flirting and seduction.

To change the perception of others regarding you to your benefit.

To rapidly gain skill regarding any artistic pursuits.

To understand the mechanics of any object, relationship, psychology, etc. for the purpose of manipulation.

6th House of Service and Health:

To create harmony between coworkers.

To be held in high esteem in one's place of work.

To achieve mastery of a desired skill.

7th House of Marriage and Partnership:

To bring clear communication and mutual understanding to a marriage or partnership.

8th House of Death and New Beginnings

To convince others to lend money to us.

9th House of Mental Exploration:

To achieve mastery of magick and occult philosophy.

To develop psychic abilities such as clairvoyance, clairaudience, etc.

To understand the nature of thought, mind, and perceptions and how they influence one's life and create change in one's environment.

10th House of Career

To achieve promotion through charm.

To influence the mind of authority figures and make them more likely to obey our will.

To elevate one's social status.

11th House of Hopes, Wishes, and Friends

To understand the collective mind of groups and sway them in your favor.

12th House of the Subconscious, Dreams, and Secrets

To transform the subconscious at will for dramatic life transformations of self or others.

To end their self-destructive behavior in self or others.

To cause others to have compassion and empathy for us.

To achieve enlightenment on any subject through a period of meditation.

Words of Power

HAH-YEE-EL

HAH-KEH-TAH-TEE-YEL

YAH-NEV-EE-VAH-EL

YAW-FAH-KET-EE-YEL

DAHN-TAH-LEE-AWN

72. ANDROMALIUS

Planetary Aspect

Moon on Earth

Applications in the 12 houses

1st House of Self:

To perceive yourself and others as they truly are.

To uncover negative or harmful traits in self and others to change them.

2nd House of Possessions:

To protect from theft.

To discover a thief and return stolen goods.

To find overlooked or rare valuables that could bring you a good profit.

3rd House of Communications:

To reveal lies and secrets others try to keep from you.

To reveal a traitor.

To know when magick is being worked against you and reflect it back on the sender.

4th House of Home:

To uncover family secrets.

To destroy negative habits and personality traits at the root.

5th House of Creativity:

To reveal cheating lovers.

To discover our hidden gifts and talents.

To reveal the true thoughts and emotions of another regarding us.

6th House of Service and Health:

To reveal those who seek to sabotage us in our workplace.

To reveal rumors regarding us.

7th House of Marriage and Partnership:

To reveal infidelity in a partner.

To encourage a partner to reveal secrets they keep from us.

8th House of Death and New Beginnings

To discover information that if acted upon could rescue us from troubled times (particularly in regard to finances).

9th House of Mental Exploration:

To reveal occult secrets.

To know the mind of another.

To know your own mind and understand what will fulfill you (your true desires in life).

10th House of Career

To uncover information that can further your career goals.

To prevent secrets from being revealed that if known, could damage your reputation and lead to your downfall.

11th House of Hopes, Wishes, and Friends

To reveal the probable future of a person or group.

To keep secrets with a group hidden from the public.

To reveal secrets of others for the purpose of reconnaissance.

12th House of the Subconscious, Dreams, and Secrets

To uncover faults within our self and correct them before they destroy us.

Words of Power

MOO-MEE-AH

MAH-LEH-KEY-EE-HAH-EL

VEH-NAH-EH-DEE-EE-TZEH-BAH-EL

MAH-KEH-VAH-KEH-VEE-YEL

AND-ROW-MAH-LEE-US

Made in United States
North Haven, CT
13 June 2023

37697453R00147